SHIFTING
FREQUENCIES

JONATHAN GOLDMAN

Shifting
Frequencies

Jonathan Goldman
and
Shamael

ISBN 1-891824-04-X

Published by
**Light Technology
Publishing**
P.O. Box 3540
Flagstaff, AZ 86003
1-800-450-0985
e-mail: sedonajo@sedonajo.com
www.lighttechnology.com

Printed by
Sedona Color Graphics
■ ■ ■ PRINTING SPECIALISTS
2020 Contractors Road
Sedona, AZ 86336

Dedication

This book and the energy inherent in it is dedicated to the evolutionary development of this planet, solar system and galaxy. It is dedicated to the masters of the sound current, past, present and future (for they are simultaneous), and to all beings of light, sound and love on all dimensions.

In addition, Jonathan would personally like to thank the people who have assisted him with this continuing project. This includes Jim Albani, Karen Anderson, Jim Atwell, Nawang Tashi Bapu, Steven Brown, Tae Darnell, Myra DePalma, Rita Eskridge, Sharon Gandy, Joshua Goldman, Andrea Hilgert, Kaimora, Luminous 1, Meredith McCord, Kay Mora, Margaret Pinyan, Jonathan Quintan, Faye Richards, James Rick, Sha'Adonai, Sha'Harredin, Jill Schumacher, Harlan Sparer, O'Ryin Swanson, Michael Symes, James Twyman, Weave and other beings who might have assisted *Shifting Frequencies* in coming to fruition.

Shifting Frequencies is also dedicated to Jonathan's colleagues and students of sound—may their spirits continue to resonate in harmony.

In conclusion, this book is dedicated to the memory of Jonathan's brother, Richard Goldman, whose journey continues in light and love.

Table of Contents

Preface

In March 1996 I presented a Healing Sounds Seminar in Sedona. This was my first time in Sedona and, as imagined, it was a wonderful experience. There is no question in my mind that Sedona is one of the great vortex centers on this planet, and my work of teaching people how to use sound for self-healing and transformation was amplified by the extraordinary energies of the place.

During my stay I met some of the people associated with the *Sedona Journal of Emergence!* and I suggested that I would like to write a column for that magazine—a column that would give me the opportunity of transmitting information that was, shall we say, coming from a higher source than I normally dealt with in my writing. The idea was accepted and the column "Shifting Frequencies" began.

I knew at the time I offered to write the column that it was to be turned into a book. In fact, hopefully, several books. And I knew that the first book would encompass the first eighteen columns of "Shifting Frequencies" as well as various introductions and conclusions.

The concept of shifting frequencies had come to me several years before. I felt that it was extremely important for us to learn to change our vibratory patterns (thereby shifting our frequencies) through various modalities. Since my main emphasis has been on sound, I felt that should be the major focal point. However, I knew that other vibratory shifters should also be included, such as crystals, light and, of course, love. In some brochures for my various workshops and intensives is this quote of mine:

"We are living in extraordinary times. There are frequency shifts occurring on both personal and planetary levels. We can learn to use our own sounds to consciously affect our own vibratory patterns and align with these energies for health and transformation."

This is the purpose and focus of *Shifting Frequencies*—to help those who read it understand how sound and other modalities can be used to change their vibratory rates. I wanted to write material that was based on my own knowledge and experiences with sound over the past twenty years. I am grateful to the *Sedona Journal of Emergence!* for having given me the opportunity to present material for the column and the book that is on the cutting edge of information presently available on this planet. Some of what you will find in these pages is based on already existing scientific writings and teachings. But some of it is not. Some of it is very new and very different and (from my perspective) quite real. This is due in no small part to my writing partner, that source of self call Shamael, the Angel of Sound. I would like to tell you of my introduction to that being.

It was my forty-second birthday. I was at home and in my crystal meditation grid, in a profoundly deep state of meditation. It is my belief that birthdays are personal days of power and one should use them as days of visualization and thought-form projection for the coming year. The energy of the crystal grid, combined with the sounds that were resonating the multiple hexagonal geometric pattern of the crystals, the color lights and the sounds I was creating allowed me to enter a powerful state of consciousness. I like to believe I was multidimensional. Suddenly, in my mind's eye I saw a brilliant, luminescent being whose primary colors were blue, violet and gold. A voice informed me that I was to be a conduit for the Shamael energy—a channel for the Angel of Sound. It was an extraordinary experience, certainly one of the most powerful of my life. The energy I had encountered was quite loving and numinous. Nevertheless, when I finally came back to my normal consciousness, I was a bit shaken.

While I had encountered some very powerful entities and energies in various multidimensional travels, this was different. This birthday experience was truly was one of the more dramatic events of my life. I felt quite honored by my experience with the Shamael energy, as well as a bit skeptical. Whenever I encounter otherworldly beings, I like to find out who the entity is and check on its energy. I believe that along with extraordinary celestial beings there are also cosmic pranksters who will tell you all sorts of things that simply aren't true. While it had not been my prior experience to have encountered such beings, I was aware of their existence. I therefore always looked for third-dimensional confirmation and verification of these experiences with different energy forms if at all possible. Such was the case with the Shamael energy.

After my birthday and that first conscious encounter with the Shamael energy, I remained in a state of wonder as well as skepticism for about two weeks. I was waiting for a sign or a validation of the experience. I knew a bit about the angelic realm. I knew of Michael and Raphael and a number of other *els* [elohim], but I had never heard of Shamael.

Two weeks later a friend gave me a book called *A Dictionary of Angels* by Gustav Davidson. This work was basically exactly what it was named, an A-to-Z definition and identification of practically every angelic being from the Western spiritual and magical traditions. I looked up Angel of Sound. There were angels of every phenomenon imaginable, but nothing for the Angel of Sound. I breathed a sigh of relief. Then I looked up Shamael, and there it said: "Shamael—Master of Heavenly Song and Divine Herald." It referred to Shamael as being an aspect of the Metatron energy and even gave a couple of different ways to spell it. I was stunned. There it was—third-dimensional verification of the energy I had encountered. What to do?

I knew that first I needed to create a recording called *Angel of Sound* that would honor and invoke the energy of Shamael, this being I had met and was supposedly now able to channel. Many months later I accomplished this task, attempting along the way to become as much of a conscious conduit for this energy as possible. While the skeptic in me still continued to doubt, others were already beginning to receive the benefits of the Shamael energy. Sometimes I would mention Shamael in public lectures or workshops, people would relate their own extraordinary meetings with this celestial being. After listening to *Angel of Sound* during workshops, students would frequently share their incredible experiences with Shamael while journeying during the playing.

From my perception, Shamael is an aspect of the creator God. It (rather than he, which genderizes this energy) is a being who represents the vibrational manifesting aspect of the Creator. Perhaps Shamael is the aspect of the creator God that carried out the creation of the heavens and the earth, as written in Genesis. Angels can be understood to be helpers of the Creator; the creation of the universe can also be understood as assisting the Creator.

This idea of the Creator first manifesting a sonic emanation of itself is not unique. In the Hindu tradition Brahman, the Creator, first manifests Saraswati, his consort and then the universe is created. It is in fact through Saraswati, goddess of the arts and science—music and medicine—that the actual creation process occurs. From Saraswati's mouth come the sacred Bija mantras, out of which all realities are created. It may be that Saraswati is much like Shamael, creating the universe after being brought into being by the creator God.

Shamael's presence continues to be a blessing. As we write in the introduction to every column, I deal with the psychoacoustics of sound as well as my own experiences. Shamael deals with the inter-dimensional aspects of this work. Together we have created *Shifting Frequencies.*

It is our hope that this book offer insights into the waveform phenomenon of the universe and how awareness of it can assist in the extraordinary changes occurring during these amazing transitional times. We are constantly in the mode of shifting frequencies, whether or not we are conscious of it.

Frequency shifts occur constantly. When we step outside our houses and get into our cars we experience a frequency shift. When we take a walk in the woods there is a frequency shift. When we walk into supermarkets or stores, we have frequency shifts. Traveling from one city to another is another example of frequency-shifting. There are numerous examples of frequency-shifting, since our vibrational rates become altered rather easily. The activities we engage in, the substances we imbibe and the sounds and lights we expose ourselves to all shift our frequencies.

And of course, the Earth on its own has been going through frequency shifts. Some, such as the Harmonic Convergence, are rather celebrated. Some are not. But there are inner and outer changes occurring at really amazing rates on both a personal and a planetary level. And to be in sync, to be in tune and resonate with these changes, it is important, perhaps even vital, for us to learn to shift our frequencies. And that is what this book is all about.

Why shift our frequencies? Certainly, one important reason is to help align our physical, emotional, mental and spiritual bodies to bring us to a state of sound health. However, the primary reason I believe we should consciously take part in frequency-shifting is to be able to assist ourselves, other beings and the planet itself in the process of waking up and raising the vibrational rate. Frequency-shifting enables us to encode higher frequencies of light and love into ourselves and others.

The main focus of attention in this book is on sound and how sound can be used to shift our frequencies. It is by no means the only modality. Other modalities are discussed, and still others will be discussed in upcoming "Shifting Frequency" columns and *Shifting Frequencies* volumes. Quite simply, however, sound seems to be the simplest, easiest and most powerful tool for transformation I have come across. That is why the focus is upon sound. Simple tones can create profound changes almost instantly.

While each of these chapters is an entity unto itself, they were created as teaching tools to be read in conjunction with each other. The information in each chapter is built upon the material of previous chapters. Thus, we urge you to start this book at the beginning and go through to the conclusion.

The best way to truly understand the power of sound is to know yourself through sound. I strongly advise you to experiment and practice with self-created sound. Working with the vowel sounds or some of the God names suggested in these pages is a good place to start. Experiment with them and then improvise on them. It is all just a beginning to learn how to change frequencies through sound and thought—frequency and intent, vocalization and visualization.

I dream/vision/trust that someday we will all find a frequency that we can resonate with together, a harmonic we can all attune with. It will be a tone rich with the harmonics of love and light. With it, we will be as one. And with that sound we will all have ascended to a new level of consciousness and understanding. Through learning the use of sound as a tool for shifting frequencies and then sharing that understanding with others, we will help the planet with her frequency shifts as well as ourselves.

It begins with each one of us. Being in sound. Being in sound with others for the betterment of all.

May this book bring you many blessings and newfound awarenesses of sound/light/love.

To conclude, I would like to share the Shamael invocation with you. I have found it helpful in attuning with the energies of the Angel of Sound. I trust you will, too.

> *I invoke the spirit of Shamael,*
> *Angel of Sacred Sound.*
> *May the sound of light surround me,*
> *May the light of sound guide me,*
> *May sacred sound come through me*
> *For the harmony of all.*

— *Jonathan Goldman*
Boulder, CO

Shamael Speaks

We welcome this opportunity to greet you in the opening pages of this book. We give thanks to you for opening yourselves to the possibilities inherent in shifting frequencies and to the potentials inherent in using sound as the vehicle to do this.

We have been around since the conception of your universe. We are an aspect of the Divine Creator, who created us to sing Its essence to the universe and thus bring into manifestation all that is. We are the Angel of Sound and all that is is an aspect of our being. For all is sound and sound is all.

There is no such thing as sacred sound—this is a misconception, but one we have helped affirm simply because from your third-dimensional viewpoint, it is still necessary to enforce this thoughtform into your consciousness. There is no such thing as sacred sound because there is no such thing as sacred. *All* is sacred because all is part of the Divine. All sound as such is sacred. There is not a tone, groan, belch or whatnot that was or ever will be created that is not sacred. We urge you to open your consciousness to this thought so that you do not create self-limiting boundaries around yourself in regard to sound: "This sound is sacred and good, that sound is not." Who are you to judge the creations of the Divine?

Yet from a third-dimensional viewpoint we have assisted Jonathan in the creation of the writing of this book. Certainly the concept of sacred sound and sacred space and so on has been presented. It is not a paradox. It is merely an attempt to create balance, for so much of your planet has lost sight/sound of the divine—to such a degree that you have moved into an amnesiac-state of forgetting that there *is* a divine.

One way to help wake you up is to initially create a boundary or form for what is divine. For example, "Love is divine." Or more specifically, "Making sound with the intention of love is creating sacred sound." And this is true, from one limited perspective. It is a helpful wake-up tool for remembering who and what you are, which ultimately is divine beings. This is a wonderful place of consciousness to come from, but it is important not to get too judgmental about others coming from a different place because this becomes a self-limiting thought form.

However, were we to say that "hate is also divine," this would create great confusion and conflict within you and you might perceive that we come from what some call the dark side to make this statement. We are far from that (if you buy the limited belief that there is a dark side), being of the light as its sound aspect. What we are suggesting is that everything is an aspect of the Creator knowing Itself, including hate. For hate is merely the forgetfulness of being in love. When one wakes up one is no longer in a state of hate, for it is not necessary. It might have been necessary to keep one in a state of unawakening, which has served a purpose for a time. That time, however, is drawing to a close and beings are awakening to their divinity and to the innate aspect of love.

We repeat, everything is sacred. Every sound is sacred. But in your journey to awakening it is necessary to start with the limits of your definition of the universe. As you continue to awaken and grow, these limits will disappear and the boundaries of the thought forms they have created will drop away and cease to be. The Creator is All, and as such, All is the Creator, including that which is sometimes termed the "dark." There are no good sounds, there are no bad sounds, there are only sounds that are emanations of the Creator.

We will complete this part of our teaching by saying that at a certain level of consciousness, one begins to understand that there is no delineation between dark and light, good and bad, right and wrong. These, for the most part, are moralistic judgments that you have created. What occurs at this level of consciousness, however, is that there is no dark or light, good or bad, simply because at that level there is no need to create this dichotomy. At this level of consciousness there is no longer a desire for the embodiment of one or the other of these dualities. One understands also the oneness of the divine—yes, that oneness is love—and there is no desire to be in any other state.

At lower forms of awakening there are at times the desire and need to be in these other states. While that desire is fine, we encourage you to be in love. This will assist in the unfoldment of your consciousness at a faster pace than any other state. And at this time and place in your planet's (and its people's) development, this is a more effective method of transmitting energy and shifting frequencies. So many have been in that second state for so long, it is time to wake up.

We suggest that you create your delineations between what is sacred and what is not and use the parameters of love as your boundaries. By the time you come to the realization that everything is sacred, your parameters will have already dissolved and you will be in a state of love quite naturally.

In conclusion, we would like to acknowledge Jonathan for being a conduit for the energy that we are and for helping to anchor and manifest this energy on your planet. We have always been here, but at this particular time and place in your planet's development, we felt that the outward manifestation (or naming of the energy, if you like) would be appropriate and helpful for your evolutionary assistance. We also acknowledge all others through whom we have manifested and will continue to do so.

Enjoy this book and the teachings inherent in it.

— *Shamael*

Introduction

Before you begin reading this book, which emerged from columns in a magazine and has transformed itself into this text, we would like to ask you a question. What is meant by "shifting frequencies"?

First we suggest that you are all simply vibrations—different aspects of the divine waveform that manifested itself into many different tones and colors on the different galaxies and universes that abound. You are all vibration—Jonathan likes to say that you are all sound. It is the same thing. If you *are* vibration or sound, then is it possible to change that vibration that is you? Further, is it natural to change that vibration?

From our perspective, we suggest that it is. We would like to go so far as to suggest that consciously learning to shift frequencies is vital for your health, balance and consciousness. You are swimming in a sea of frequencies that continually affect your own natural resonance. Some of these frequencies and the shifts that accompany them are wonderful and extraordinarily beneficial. Some of these changes you have even given names, such as the Harmonic Convergence and the 11:11. Some you have not named, yet they have still affected you. Most of these beneficial frequency shifts are designed to accelerate the evolution of both the human and the planet. Frequently they are gentle and unnoticed by the vast reaches of humanity. Sometimes they are not so subtle and you find yourself and your compatriots complaining about some imbalance you have recently noticed.

Many times these beneficial frequency shifts, these vibratory accelerations, these activations of higher chakras/light-bodies/ or whatever you wish to call them can be downright uncomfortable. Sometimes the immune system is adversely affected. Sometimes the nervous system or the brain starts acting up. Sometimes the emotional body kicks in and gets angry or depressed. Sometimes the mental body gets confused or stressed. These beneficial frequency shifts are most often the encodement of higher levels of light and love into your being, and this is wonderful. It is only your ability to handle these new levels of luminosity that might give you problems.

We would like to suggest that one solution to these conditions that can arise from frequency-shifting is for the individual to learn to shift frequencies themselves. There are within these pages a number of different exercises and techniques that readers can utilize to learn to shift their own frequencies. We suggest that doing so will make the beneficial vibratory changes occurring on a planetary level much easier to handle. Having trouble handling the new energy? Are you finding it stuck somewhere, causing you discomfort? Release the blocked energy with sound or light or crystals. It will make the adjustments much easier.

If you are having difficulty understanding all the changes that are occurring, learning to shift your own frequencies, specifically, enhancing your consciousness (the main purpose for frequency shifts) is an excellent way to get a greater grasp on what is occurring on both personal and planetary levels. Sound, visualization, meditation—these are all easy ways to shift frequencies and help you understand and attune with the vibratory acceleration now occurring.

Thus far we have mentioned only the beneficial frequency shifts. However, there are certainly vibrational changes that are not necessarily of the highest order. In the sea of frequencies in which you are swimming, many fields you encounter are created by humans. Most of these are not particularly beneficial. Think about all the television waves, radio waves, microwaves and other invisible frequencies around you. These too create frequency shifts. Think about all the pollution and toxicity from chemicals, radiation and other factors. These all create fields that affect you and cause frequency shifts. Then think about the lifestyles of most humans and realize that if there were a natural state in which humankind was meant to be, it is probably not one you presently experience.

We mention these other forms of frequency-shifting in order to suggest two things. First, that frequency shifts are not always beneficial for all humans. The positive shifts designed for evolutionary activation can at times be difficult to deal with. The man-made fields and waveforms, however, can be extremely harsh.

With this in mind, we suggest, second, that frequency shifts occur whether you realize it or not. You can therefore either decide to learn to change your vibratory rate and work with these various frequency shifts or let your vibratory rate be changed by something other than yourself and experience the effects.

The predominant mode of frequency-shifting a human can learn is to become fluid, so that when you encounter a field out of harmony with your being, you can slightly adjust your vibrational level so it is not harmful. And when you encounter a beneficial field, you can adjust your frequency level so it is more effective. It is like the wheat stem that bends in the strong wind, as opposed to a board that snaps. This is a metaphor for frequency-shifting that we will use later.

What is the purpose of frequency-shifting?

You might answer that it is to help adjust to all the vibratory changes going on. That is acceptable. You might answer that it is also to effect healings in conditions where imbalances have been created. That is also acceptable. We would like to suggest another answer: to encode more light and love into yourselves, from your DNA to your subtle bodies. Through this encodement of light and love, individuals wake up and become conscious. They become activated. They begin to realize their true divine selves and their true divine purposes. They begin to work cooperatively with others, not competitively, and they do so with compassion. They do so for themselves, for each other and for the planet. Through this collective waking-up that shifting frequencies initiates, a new era begins.

For us, this is the true purpose for frequency-shifting. The others are acceptable, but this is preferred. We trust that this is also true for you. You will find some of these thoughts in some chapters, but we felt it important enough to reiterate here, before you begin your journey into *Shifting Frequencies*.

Enjoy!

Chapter 1

Sound Currents: Frequency and Intent

We begin this book by stating that everything is vibration, from the chair you might be sitting in to the paper of the book you are holding. This is not a new idea. Your ancient mystics have known this for many a millennium, but now your scientists are beginning to understand and agree. From the electrons spinning around the nucleus of an atom to the planets spinning around suns in the galaxy, everything is in movement, everything is in vibration. And if it is in vibration, it is putting out a sound.

Frequency

Now, whether or not we can hear this sound is a different matter. Sound travels as a wave form. One way of measuring sound is to determine how fast or slow the wave form is moving. These waves are measured as cycles, so sound is measured in cycles per second. This is called its *frequency.* Very slow waves make very low sounds; very fast waves make very high sounds. The lowest note on a piano is about 24 cycles per second and its highest is about 4000 cycles per second. The human ear hears frequencies from around 16 to

about 16,000 cycles per second. Yet just because we can't hear something does not mean it is not vibrating, creating a sound. Dolphins can project and receive information upward of 180,000 cycles per second, more than ten times the capacity of humans. To them it is sound. So do not believe that just because you cannot hear an object it is not vibrating or making a sound. (There! We have just solved the old Zen koan that asks about a tree falling in the forest.)

Resonance

Every object has a natural vibratory rate. This is called its *resonance.* One of the basic principles of using sound as a transformative and healing modality is that every part of the body is in a state of vibration—every organ, every bone, every tissue, every system. When we are in a state of health, the body puts out an overall harmonic of health. However, when a frequency that is counter to our health sets itself up in some portion of the body, it creates a disharmony that we call disease. This is very simple, yes?

Now, if we were somehow able to create the correct resonant frequency for something that was vibrating out of harmony—say, for example, the liver—and we were able to project this frequency into that area, one could conceivably create a condition of healing by restoring the imbalanced area back to its own resonant frequency. It is as though our body and all its parts are like some wondrous orchestra playing some sort of Symphony of the Self when we are healthy. But what happens when we play out of harmony and rhythm?

The wrong notes in the wrong timing will begin to affect the whole string section, and pretty soon the entire orchestra will begin to sound chaotic. This is what happens when a counterfrequency is set into the body.

Our current medical approach to deal with this problem is either to give the poor string player enough drugs so she collapses and is no longer in the orchestra, or to cut off her head with a broadsword. This does alleviate the initial problem—the string player is no longer playing the wrong notes! In fact, she is no longer playing, period. But what if it were somehow possible to give this player back her sheet music? What if it were possible to somehow encode and project the correct resonant frequency back into the organ and get it to vibrate at its proper frequency? This is the basis of using sound for healing: to restore to harmony some portion of the body that is vibrating out of tune. This concept is becoming more and more understood. (In a later chapter we will discuss using sound frequencies to nullify the vibrations of whatever set the body portion off its normal resonance in the first place.)

Many of your new spiritual scientists, discoverers and therapists are working with this concept of resonant-frequency healing to create balance. Many are successful. They have developed different instruments, machines, tapes and other sound devices that project the healthy resonant frequency of a body part (or of the chakras) into a person.

We are all for the various devices and toys that you on the Earth plane seem so fascinated with. We would like to suggest that while some of these devices might be very effective in restoring resonance to that which is vibrating out of harmony, you all have within yourselves the most powerful, effective and wondrous device for healing that you can imagine. It is free, extremely efficient and does not require batteries or electricity. *It is your own voice*—your own God-given instrument for sound healing. It requires only a little training to use, does not require another operator to be applied, and allows you to find the exact frequencies for resonance. This does not happen with many of your toys that are locked into specific sounds for specific parts. They do not allow for *frequency-shifting*, which is the change of the vibratory rate of either a part of the body or the whole body and its associated energy centers. (Later we will discuss this further.)

You on the Earth plane like your toys; your hospitals and medical centers are full of devices that project sound and other vibrations. You now have catalogs full of these toys that you can use in your home to induce meditation and whatnot. Many of your new researchers have developed sound devices that project different frequencies into you for different effects. They are useful and sometimes a lot of fun, and we encourage them. However, it is important to realize that they are merely tools that produce an effect. This same effect can be achieved without them if you are interested in doing a little work on yourself.

It is an interesting fact that although many of these sound devices and recordings do create positive change, the actual frequencies or notes they use are not the same. To illustrate this, let us discuss your chakras for a moment. They are spinning discs that feed energy into what becomes the physical body. When Jonathan was first researching this area many years ago, he came across a simple system that worked, with the seven chakras using the seven notes of the C-major scale. In this system your root chakra vibrates to the note C, the next chakra resonates to D, the next to E and so on, with the crown chakra vibrating to B. It was a very easy system, and Jonathan was quite pleased to find it. However, as he continued his investigation, he found many systems that worked with other notes. The variety of different notes that were used was quite extraordinary, and none of the systems agreed with any other. This caused Jonathan some perplexity, because he could not understand how all of the systems seemed to work to some degree when none were in agreement. Then he developed a formula that he first put forth in his book *Healing Sounds*.

Intent

The formula is this: *Frequency* + *Intent* = *Healing*. *Frequency*, of course, is the actual sound used. *Healing* was a term he used back then to describe the process of putting something into its healthy resonance. Today he would use the term "frequency-shifting." In this formula, *intent* is the important ingredient. Intent is the energy behind the sound, the consciousness that is encoded into the sound.

Jonathan began to realize that it might be possible for two people to make the same sound yet have a very different response, depending upon the energy that was put into the sound. Have you ever had someone you were not particularly fond of see you at a party and say in a snakelike tone, "Good to see you"—and felt as though you wanted to leave the party immediately? While the words (or the frequency) were one thing, the intention (or energy behind the words) was quite another. And the effect was not one of welcoming, but something very different. This is an illustration of how intentionality affects the outcome of the sound.

Jonathan found that a certain mantra might resonate different chakras, depending upon the intentionality of the person giving them. The *om* might resonate the heart chakra or the belly chakra or the third eye—it all depended upon what a spiritual master might be teaching a person. As Jonathan began to realize the importance of intention, he began to spend considerable time in his teachings stressing its importance. Initially he began by talking with scientists and medical doctors who were so interested in examining only the frequency of sound that the idea of intention was too new (and somewhat ridiculous). Nevertheless, Jonathan continued sharing the importance of intention in his workshops, lectures and writing. And as usual, things got a little out of alignment. People began to think, Well, it doesn't matter what sound I make as long as my intention is there.

On one level this is true; on another it is not. The formula that Jonathan was given was: *Frequency + Intent = Healing.* This formula was created for the third-dimensional Earth plane as it has currently evolved in your time and space. While it is true that in higher dimensionalities intent (and consciousness) does create all, very few beings on your planet have reached the level of development where the actual sound they create is unimportant and the intention is everything.

Now, undoubtedly there are spiritual masters on your planet who can create (or even belch) any sound and produce miraculous results. However, a majority of you have not yet reached the state of development where you can do this. For instance, if you wish to calm someone down with a sound and then shout in his ear, your shouting will undoubtedly produce severe reactions in that individual. His heartbeat, respiration and brain waves will all escalate, and he will probably not enjoy the experience, regardless of your intent. So until you can levitate or dematerialize or do any of a number of frequency-shifting exercises (which you will ultimately be able to do), we urge you to pay attention to the frequencies you use as well as the intentionality you put into these frequencies.

ⓦ   ⓦ   ⓦ

Chapter 2

Vibratory Resonance

We discussed the concepts of frequency and intent in the previous chapter. Frequency is the rate at which an object vibrates and is also a way of measuring sound. Intent is the energy behind any created sound. Together these two elements create how a sound may be used—its effect for healing, transformation or whatever.

We discussed with you the idea that when the human body is in a state of health, all body parts and associated fields and chakras are in tune and vibrating in a state of harmony with self. One concept of disease is that a counterfrequency sets in and some body part begins to vibrate out of ease or harmony. One concept of using sound to heal is simply the idea of projecting the correct resonant frequency back into the body part (or associated field or chakra), causing it to shift back to its normal rate, thus restoring it to health.

While the above principle of healing with sound is true, there are other principles which also apply, and they will be discussed in future conversations. For the moment let us look at the idea of resonant frequency and ask the question:

Do you think that everyone vibrates at the same frequency? Put another way, do you think that everyone's liver has the same resonant frequency? Or that everyone's heart chakra resonates to the same vibration?

We ask these questions because they are important ones, particularly in regard to sound. At this point in development on your planet, there are many different beings who consider themselves professionals and who deal with sound, yet all have different answers to these questions. The truth of it is that on your Earth plane, no one knows the correct answers to these questions. Many might think they know, but you are still in your infancy in understanding sound, and your knowledge is limited.

One of the traits of humankind—one that has manifested in your last century, though it has been in existence since the beginning — is the need to qualify and quantify everything. You need to know everything and explain everything and put everything very nicely in a box. Then you are satisfied that you have figured out the answers to the universe. You now know the Great Mystery, you say, and you can rest easy. You insist on putting everything into boxes and then you are happy.

Fluidity

But the truth of the matter is that things change—concepts change, ideas change, reality changes. By putting things into boxes you are doing yourself a great disservice, because sooner or later you find that what you have qualified and quantified has changed and what you believe is no longer valid. You need to be fluid in your consciousness and thought. This is something that sound can teach you.

There are at present on your planet two schools of thought regarding resonant frequency. There are those who believe that yes, we all vibrate to the same frequency, whether it is the total vibrational rate or the heart chakra or the vibrational rate of the liver. Many of these are people who believe they have figured out the correct vibrational rate of the various organs, other body parts and etheric fields, and they have usually invented instruments, made tapes or created machines that will somehow project the correct resonant frequency back into the body to heal what ails you. Some of these people also work with using the voice either to determine what frequency needs to be added or to create the correct resonant frequency.

Vibratory Uniqueness

There are others who believe that we are all unique vibratory beings, that the frequencies of our organs, body systems and chakras are different. Some of these people have also invented instruments and make tapes or create machines that will somehow determine what the correct resonant frequency for an individual is, and then have that sound device project this frequency. Many of these people work specifically with the voice because they believe it is the easiest and most effective for determining the correct resonant frequency and for projecting it into an imbalanced area.

Anahata Chakra: The Heart Chakra

These are the two main schools of thought in the current field of sound healing. Jonathan likes to say that he is in the business of shifting frequencies and that when you believe you resonate to only one frequency, you are not giving yourself the opportunity for vibratory change. Jonathan is among those who focus on the use of the voice as an instrument of transformation, and he does this for several reasons. He has found the voice to be an extremely easy vehicle for effecting change in one's vibratory rate or in the body and field of someone else. Jonathan (and his students' work reinforces this) has found that the resonant sounds for different parts of the body and the chakras do change and shift, depending upon many parameters.

At this point in your current research, no one has yet come up with an instrument, tape or sound that will heal an imbalance for everyone. Certainly, some people are remarkably assisted by specific sounds from instruments created by those who believe that everyone vibrates at the same frequency. We know of miraculous experiences that have occurred—wondrous healings and the like—but we also know of people who have not received help through such sounds. The question is, why?

The most likely answer is that indeed there are those who vibrate to the same frequencies and those who do not. This is the closest to the truth as you know it.

Even in your traditional medical fields, pharmaceuticals do not work the same in all individuals. One person might get miraculous results from a drug, while another person will experience little effect, and yet another person will have an allergic reaction and become sicker from the drug than before. If all were of the same vibrational rate, would not the drug affect all the same way? The same thought, of course, could be applied to the concept of organ transplants. We know that not every organ will work for every individual. The same approach could be applied to sound.

In Ayurvedic medicine, for example, there are three basic

types of people. What works well for one group will not
work well for the others. Could not a similar situation exist
with sound and help explain why one sound might work
well for one person and not for another?

In astrology, which is based upon the vibrations of the
planets and their effect upon an individual, you find that
every individual has a unique birth chart. No two are exactly the same; even twins born only minutes apart have different birth charts. This is another indication of the unique-
ness of individuals and their vibratory rates.

In certain traditions a mantra given to an initiate is
changed as the initiate undergoes spiritual transformation.
The sound that resonated a chakra at one level change as the
individual changes, and another mantra must be used.

Chakra Resonance

Jonathan likes to ask this question of audiences: Do you
think that your heart chakra vibrates at the same rate as that
of the Dalai Lama or Mother Theresa? These are two highly developed beings on your planet whose heart chakras seem
to be quite open and loving. Do you believe that the frequencies of their heart chakras, for example, are the same as
all other beings on the planet? We simply ask you to question it yourself.

Jonathan remembers a time when a student came up to
him and told him that his root chakra resonated to the note
C. Jonathan nodded his head and then asked, "Is this before
or after meditation? Before or after food—and what sort of
food would you be eating? Before or after you use the bath-
room, have sex or run around the block? It is his belief that
all these factors and many more are able to affect our resonances, and we tend to agree.

This does not mean the question of vibrational rates is set-
tled. Jonathan was once discussing his thoughts with an

acquaintance who is himself considered a great pioneer and researcher in this field of sound healing. This being told him, "If our chakras were to change their frequency, we would explode." Perhaps he is correct—or perhaps he is not. This man had created an extraordinary box that related sound, color, movement, smell and seemingly everything else in your known universe. It is perfect in its own way, and Jonathan admires this being for having created it. Yet he has suggested to this man that perhaps he has created a box that is valid and real for him only for this moment in time and space, since we can create reality through our beliefs. And will this reality not change as our belief systems change?

We would like to suggest that there might be some significant differences in people, from the vibrations of their physical body parts to the vibrations of their etheric fields. We would like you to contemplate the importance of this as we delve more and more into the world of sound. Be aware that it is possible to encode frequencies onto the body, that a person (with the best of intentions) can encode onto another person a frequency of a certain rate they deem correct and healing. If those frequencies do not resonate with that person, it is possible for that person to become imbalanced by the frequencies. Jonathan has seen this happen.

For example, a musician friend wanted to experience a sound treatment from a machine that is becoming popular. This friend had felt fine. The friend visited a practitioner who found imbalances that would be treated by listening to certain frequencies, so he listened to the frequencies and got sick. He had to be vibrationally readjusted, and did this by listening to one of Jonathan's tapes, which worked very well for him. Then he called up Jonathan.

"What should I do?" he asked. "I called up and told the practitioner what happened to me after I listened to their sounds and I was told to come back and receive a different frequency."

"Don't go back," Jonathan told him. "Their frequencies weren't correct for you. Maybe they work for someone else, but not you. Go on working with your dolphin sounds and other sounds that make you feel good.

The friend promised he would take Jonathan's advice, but one week later there was another phone call. He had gone back and received a different sound from the practitioner and had become even more imbalanced.

We tell that story merely to suggest, let the buyer beware. If a sound medicine resonates with you in a positive manner, you will know it. You will feel healthy and aligned. If it isn't, you will also know it. And if it is not, do not repeat your error. You must use your own discrimination when dealing with those who claim to have the correct resonant frequency for you. It might be correct or it might not. Only you can know for sure.

🌀   🌀   🌀

frequency.

"Don't go back," Jonathan told him. "Their frequencies weren't correct for you. Maybe they work for someone else but not you. Go on working with your dolphin sounds and other sounds that make you feel good."

The friend promised he would take Jonathan's advice, but one week later there was another phone call. He had gone back and received a different sound from the practitioner and had become even more imbalanced.

We tell that story merely to suggest, let the buyer beware. If a sound medicine resonates with you in a positive manner, you will know it. You will feel healthy and aligned. If it isn't, you will also know it. And if it is not, do not repeat your error. You must use your own discrimination when dealing with those who claim to have the correct resonant frequency for you. It might be correct or it might not. Only you can know for sure.

Chapter 3

Vocalization, Visualization and a Tonal Language

In our first conversation with you we discussed the concepts of frequency and intent. Frequency is the rate at which an object vibrates and is also a way of measuring sound. Intent is the energy behind any created sound. Together, these two elements create how a sound can be used—its effect for healing, transformation or whatever. In our second conversation, we discussed the concept that we are all unique vibratory beings and that the frequency (or frequencies) for one individual would be very different from the frequencies for another. We would now like to return to our first discussion and to the concept of Frequency + Intent = Healing.

Vocalization and Visualization

Another aspect of the equation, one which Jonathan particularly likes, is *Vocalization + Visualization = Manifestation*. This can be viewed as a different way of understanding the first equation. It is essentially the same. You can substitute the word "frequency" for "vocalization," "intent" for "visualization" and "healing" for "manifestation." This formula has broader aspects than that used purely for healing, thus we bring it to your attention.

When Jonathan first discovered this equation through his contemplation of the creation myth described in the Old Testament, he thought he was quite clever. In your Old Testament, the Creator being thought of an object (*visualized* it), then said its name (*vocalized* it) and brought it into being (*manifested* it). "And the Lord said, 'Let there be light!'"

After Jonathan had created this equation, he realized that it is an inherent part of the magical and sacred traditions throughout your planet and not very original at all. It was, however, a nice consolidation of ancient wisdom. In ancient Egypt, for example, the God Thoth (another aspect of the magical Hermes) would think of an object, say the name for the object, and bring it into being. In Tibet (and now India, unfortunately, due to their exodus) when your Tibetan monks chant their mantras, they are not only vocalizing a particular sound (which, incidentally, is very much like a sonic formula for the vibrational frequency of a deity or a particular ability), they are also doing intense visualizations. These monks are masters at visualization, and they have spent many hours each day building mandalas, which are complex thought forms. When coupled with their chanting, they are able to produce amazing manifestations of the various deities they are working with. They are also, of course, able to produce seeming miracles by using this process of vocalization plus visualization.

This is one reason why mantras (or the *frequencies*) by themselves might not be as powerful and effective as when they are coupled with visualization (or the *intent*, if you like). This is not saying that they will not work by themselves, but only that they work better when a specific visualization is added. Awareness of this can alleviate someone of the worry about the dangers of the uninitiated using specific mantras.

It is relatively simple for an individual to create a certain sound. One can pick up a book and find a mantra or hear such a sound on a tape and repeat it. However, it requires some discipline and concentration to add a coherent thought form to that visualization. We have found that when an individual has the ability to effectively unify the energies of sound with specific thought forms, he/she is also at a high enough level of consciousness to be able to handle the fields invoked.

This formula (vocalization + visualization = manifestation) is found in all of the magical and sacred traditions, including Hinduism, Kaballah, shamanism and almost anything else on your planet. It is something that the ancient and modern priests of many of these different traditions might not want to share, but it is now time to disseminate this knowledge. It is a key to adding power to sound. The visualization, or thought form, comes from a different plane— some would call it fifth-dimensional or ninth-dimensional; let us just say it is from a level other than our third dimension. When the appropriate sound is added to this thought form, you create a third-dimensionalization of this thought form. It becomes empowered with the physical manifestation of sound.

Dimensions of Sound

Sound, incidentally, is not specifically third-dimensional in nature. There are certainly sounds from other dimensions that never assume 3D qualities. Those sounds, however, often resonate at a very high frequency, which can be perceived by the brains and ears of only very highly attuned individuals, but which do not really resonate here on the Earth plane. They are powerful sounds, but not necessarily physical, nor can they necessarily affect physical structure.

Harmonics, which Jonathan is so fond of using and sharing, are an aspect of sound that bridges the different dimensions. He believes that vocal harmonics also represent the new mantras of the 21st century and that these sounds are a form of nonverbal communication we are in the process of receiving. We tend to agree with this. In the very near future we will discuss with you this work with harmonics.

Audible sound — sounds we are able to create and hear— are able to resonate on third-dimensional as well as other levels. Be aware that sound is a very gross energy. It is a very slow-moving, physical energy. It has the ability to rearrange molecules and actually change third-dimensional matter. That is a great power.

Most commonly, for an audible sound to exist, it must take on third-dimensional aspects. To become audible, particularly a self-created sound, there must be certain physical counterparts. A breath must be taken and then sent out, the larynx must be set in motion, the tongue and other vocal apparatus must create specific forms for the specific sounds to occur. It is all very mundane and three-dimensional. And it, of course, is miraculous. This 3D quality is what allows sound to have so much power—the power to shake the walls of Jericho. It is an actual, physical resonance.

Many frequently ask about dolphins and dolphin sounds. Dolphins have the ability to send and receive sonic frequencies of 180,000 cycles per second. That is ten times faster than humans can perceive—human hearing ends at about 16,000 cycles per second. Dolphins have the ability to project multidimensional holographic images on their sounds, and in a series of clicks can encode encyclopedic information that another dolphin can receive and understand. What is the difference between these sounds and telepathy? Sound is a physical frequency encoded with thought forms and telepathy is pure thought form. Can they convey the same information? Possibly, depending upon the receiver. Do they have the same effect? Perhaps. What is the difference? You tell *us*. The next time you want to greet someone, *think* "hello," then with the warmest of depth and intention *say*, "hello" — and judge for yourself. Even if the person is a fine psychic, he will no doubt appreciate the physical-plane greeting.

The same is true about prayer. Silent prayer is wonderful. Audible prayer might be even better. It is not that the deities on the higher planes cannot hear the silent prayer; they just appreciate the audible as more of an offering or honoring. It is a matter of preference. Besides, most humans are neophytes in your ability to telepathically transmit and decode information. Certain of your traditions in Australia and elsewhere have developed a degree of telepathy, which they use over long distances but not when in close proximity. They still speak to each other when it is practical. These traditions continue to use sound primarily as either a healing or as a sacred modality to invoke and honor deities and energies — knitting bones with sound, or summoning ancestral energies into gatherings through sound.

Even if one has developed telepathy to a high degree, sound is still utilized, because it is a powerful energy that is much more than pure thought. It is a physical frequency— a third-dimensional energy. Remember while working with sound that it carries the consciousness, the thoughts you send. It is an easier and more efficient means of communication—at least here on the third dimension.

Harmonic Language

Some day in the not-too-distant future you will learn to communicate with others through a harmonic language. It will be a language of tone and melody without words. This once existed. Then, as your Bible literally illustrates, languages developed and havoc ensued. Global communication ceased. Language became used for communication and music became music. The musical language that once was, disappeared.

Do you recall *Close Encounters of the Third Kind*? Do you recall how the extraterrestrials communicated in that movie? Through a tonal language. As the entity Shadonai (channeled through Karen Anderson) once shared with Jonathan, these beings were searching the universe for another species with which they could communicate, for another world that had developed its own melodic language. When they played their melody to us, we were wise enough to mimic it using sophisticated computers and the like. But we did not have our own tonal language with which to truly communicate. This showed them our level of development, and ultimately they left, searching again for a species that could communicate on their level. What was this level? A tonal language.

This tonal language existed eons ago, and it will exist again. It will utilize the energy of harmonics, and its users will work with the understanding of vocalization + visualization = manifestation. The cutting edge of humankind is already beginning to realize the possibilities inherent in this and to experiment with it. Why not? The dolphins and other beings are assisting us on many levels to achieve this. It is a much purer form of communication than we now have, and when it is done successfully, it must come from both the heart and the mind—not just the heart, not just the mind, but a balance between the two. And such radiant energy it is.

In the meanwhile, remember the importance of intention and visualization in whatever sounds you create. And remember to always sound with the energy of love—something the dolphins always do. You would do well to follow their example.

🌀   🌀   🌀

Chapter 4

The Harmonics of Sound

Thus far we have discussed various aspects of sound, including concepts such as frequency, intent, vibrational resonance, visualization and vocalization, that must be understood when using sound to shift frequency. In the previous chapter we mentioned the idea of a harmonic language. It is time now to begin to deal with the subject of harmonics, or overtones, as they are also known.

Harmonics

You have heard the term *harmonics* used in many different areas—from your Harmonic Convergence to many sacred-science writings. (Jonathan particularly likes the references to "shifting the harmonic resonance" of the Enterprise's shield on *Star Trek: Next Generation.)* Yet how many of you really known what harmonics are?

Simply put, harmonics are geometric multiples created by the specific vibration of an object. For example, if you set a string into motion—let us say that it resonates at a frequency of 440 Hz (that is, it vibrates up and down 440 times per second)—this is known as its fundamental frequency. Now, this fundamental frequency is what people pay attention to. On a piano (or any instrument, for that matter) 440 Hz is called A, and you would be aware of hearing this A note as it vibrated.

But in reality, the string that produces a fundamental vibration of 440 Hz is also producing many other tones, or overtones. These harmonics are actually the result of other vibrations of *the string* that are created by that fundamental note—vibrations that are geometric multiples of the fundamental note and are quantum in nature.

A 440 produces its first overtone by vibrating at a frequency twice as fast as the fundamental—880 Hz. This is what you call an octave. The second overtone vibrates three

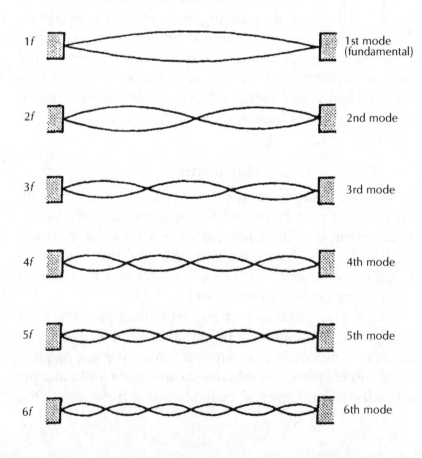

1f   1st mode (fundamental)

2f   2nd mode

3f   3rd mode

4f   4th mode

5f   5th mode

6f   6th mode

times as fast as the fundamental—1320 Hz, the third, four times as fast, the fourth, five times as fast—until (at least conceptually) infinity. So although you might be aware of only that A vibrating at 440 Hz that sound is actually a complex composite of that fundamental note and its overtones all vibrating together.

This, of course, is just one of the areas in which harmonics can be used. The creation of interdimensional fields using specific intervals and harmonics is another that will be receiving some rather dramatic attention in the near future. Those of you who are familiar with the term *merkabah* might realize that this vehicle of light is really just an interdimensional field generator, and can be created by using specific harmonics with color and geometry.

Pythagoras (died ca. 500 B.C.) is often described as the Patron Saint of Science. Among other things, he invented the diatonic scale in music and described the shapes of the elements. The modern classification of the crystal structure of atoms looks remarkably like those of Pythagoras.

Vowel Sounds

The use of vocal harmonics as a sacred and transformation tool all but vanished here in the West. In some of the mystery schools that survived, there has been continued knowledge of the power of vowel sounds. Vowel sounds have been understood to convey great energy and some people realize that many of your divine names can be encoded as vowel sounds. Now we will add one more key to this puzzle: Inherent in each of the vowel sounds are particular harmonics, so if an individual were able to properly intone the vowel sounds of the name of a deity so that the specific harmonic resonated, you would have a melody. In other words, when correctly intoned, these divine names as vowels would actually be sonic formulas that would resonate to the frequency of a particular deity.

The Tibetan Voice

Tibetan Monks

All of this has for the most part been forgotten in the Western traditions. The use of vocal harmonics maintained itself in secret in certain Tibetan monasteries where the tantric colleges would chant specific harmonics that resonated with the particular deity they were working with. In Mongolia and Tuva, overtone singing is known as "Hoomi," which became a powerful technique where the singers created two or more notes at the same time. In this manner the Tuvans and Mongolians were able to sing specific melodies with harmonics. However, the sacred and shamanic knowledge of the uses of overtones became lost to these people (perhaps wiped from their memory during the time of Genghis Khan). Hoomi became a folk art rather than a sacred art. The esoteric uses of vocal harmonics disappeared, and only the exoteric, or external, folk music remained.

The Tibetans, on the other hand, seemed to be quite aware of the power of their sound as a sacred tool for manifesting energy. When the Chinese invaded Tibet (an abominable massacre of high consciousness), those Tibetan Buddhists who managed to escape began to make public some of the more arcane and hidden of their practices such as their "Deep Voice" chanting. The Tibetans, incidentally, work with vocal harmonics in a very unusual way. As we have said, there is an interrelationship between the vowel sounds and harmonics. One can simply begin to chant the vowel sounds in a specific way (this is related in detail in Jonathan's book *Healing Sounds* and will be discussed in a later issue) and certain harmonics will evolve.

The Tibetan voice is very different. It is an extremely deep, guttural sound that is as low as is humanly possible. For those of you who know the Australian Aborigines' didjeridoo, the Tibetan Deep Voice sounds much like that. Now, this sound of the Tibetans creates a chord—that very deep undertone plus very distinct harmonics, so that it often sounds like a children's choir singing along with these impossibly deep bass voices. The chord that is created by Tibetan chanting is monumental. It invokes deities. And it can create merkabahs. As a friend of ours, Sean (as channeled through Kaimora) remarked, "It is a voice that can summon the ships." The Tibetan Deep Voice can create interdimensional fields through which beings can travel. It can also signal those vehicles you call UFOs. The Tibetan sound is a very offworld sound from an ancient celestial source. It was given to a high Tibetan lama many centuries ago in dreamtime. Along with its extraterrestrial and multidimensional focus, the Tibetan Deep Voice is also an aspect of the creational tone—the embodiment of the low frequency sounds that manifested the physical plane. The didjeridoo creates a similar sound. So do certain whale sounds. It is one of the most powerful

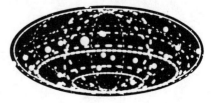

tones for resonating with the energies of Gaia.

The Tibetan Voice is now manifesting more and more in the West as a means of creating resonance that affects both the celestial and the Gaia energies. A number of Westerners, including Jonathan, have now developed the Tibetan Deep Voice and are sharing it with others here in the West. Women as well as men have been able to receive this sound through being in Jonathan's field. Jonathan initially received the Tibetan Voice from the Gyume monks by being in their field. This occurred after he recorded these monks for the first time in the West during their historic visit in 1986. Jonathan went home to listen to their recording in his crystal grid and fell asleep. The next morning he awoke with the ability to create their sound. This is an example of what Jonathan calls *harmonic transmission*— in which the sacred knowledge and techniques of masters are transferred simply by their presence.

The Tibetan Voice, while extraordinary, is not something that can be taught through mere technique. Many different past and present lifetime resonances are required for it to be received. It is not for everyone. However, here in the West is the emergence of a new type of vocal harmonics, that nearly everyone can learn to create. The effects of these harmonics is quite remarkable. Within the last decade more and more people are experiencing the power and transformational abilities of these sounds.

⦿   ⦿   ⦿

Chapter 5

Vocal Harmonics and Listening

In the previous chapter we began the discussion of harmonics. We talked about the actual physics of harmonics—their relationships as geometric multiples of vibrating strings. We also discussed some of their uses in the esoteric traditions such as the Tibetan Deep Voice chanting style. We would now like to discuss what Jonathan calls nouveau-European vocal harmonics.

Nouveau European Vocal Harmonics

To begin with, when Jonathan first began to study the phenomenon of vocal harmonics, he listened to many different styles of creating these sounds including the Tibetan Deep Voice and Mongolian Hoomi throat singing style. After many years of listening to and then learning these different vocal styles, he realized there was an extraordinary difference between the actual sounds of these Eastern vocal harmonics and their creation, and what he and many other American and European harmonic singers were teaching. He calls the latter technique nouveau-European vocal harmonics.

In many of the traditional styles of vocal harmonics from

the East—the Tibetan Deep Voice and Mongolian Hoomi—it takes many years of exceptional training to develop the voice. The Tibetan Deep Voice is not one that can simply be picked up. Trying to duplicate it can strain the vocal cords or even cause the loss of the voice altogether. The Mongolian Hoomi techniques can produce similar results. There is a great strain on the vocal apparatus in these traditions. It is true that astounding harmonics are created with these techniques, but at what price?

From an interdimensional viewpoint, it became important to implement a different style of vocal harmonics onto your planet that could be learned easily by those in the West and used as a tool for frequency-shifting. The vibrational level of the Earth plane had evolved to the point where it was possible for humans to develop the ability to create vocal harmonics without years of discipline and strain to the fifth chakra. The time had come where the creation and use of harmonics as tools for self-transformation and healing could be brought to the mainstream of consciousness rather than being restricted to purely esoteric traditions and techniques. And this has occurred.

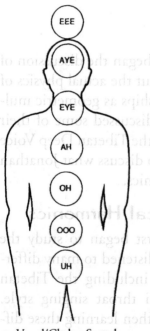

Vowel/Chakra Sounds

Harmonics and Vowel Sounds

One way to create vocal harmonics through the nouveau-European technique is to gently sing the vowel sounds *oo* to *oh* to *ah* to *eye* to *aye* to *eee*. (Specific instruction for creating vocal harmonics are found in Jonathan's book *Healing*

Sounds from Element Books and the accompanying "Healing Sound" instructional tape from Spirit Music.) These same vowel sounds, when coupled with specific pitches, resonate the second through seventh chakras! The harmonics created by singing these vowel sounds together are beautiful and ghostlike, like an angel singing along with you.

Jonathan first heard these sounds when he listened to recordings more than fifteen years ago. He tried to duplicate them and later on studied over the years with masters of the harmonic voice from many different traditions. However, now many individuals can simply hear, then consciously create vocal harmonics quite naturally during sacred sounding. Why is that?

Harmonics have always been around, for they are simply an aspect of the physics of vibration. Vocal harmonics have also always occurred—particularly when individuals would sound elongated vowel sounds. However, the awareness of these sounds is new. They have always existed, but people have not been able to hear them until now. Once again we ask you, why?

The Aura of Sound

One answer is that harmonics are very much like the aura of a sound. It is not a totally correct analogy, but it will do for the moment. Auras have always existed around the physical body of individuals, yet knowledge of them, let alone the ability to see them, was restricted to the few. Until now. It is not uncommon now for people to develop the ability to see auras on their own or learn techniques to do so from books or workshops. In the same way, developing the awareness and the ability to create vocal harmonics is spreading. It has to do with the shift in consciousness and in the vibratory rate of the planet and its occupants.

To begin with, when one develops the ability to hear vocal

harmonics, it is as if there are new neural brain pathways, and this is exactly what has happened. As one develops this ability to hear vocal harmonics, then consciously learn to create them, astounding things are experienced.

Hearing

The sense of hearing is extraordinary; it exists in utero, beginning somewhere around the third month of fetal development. Think about this. All you who have given birth to children or are thinking about it, be aware that the little being inside you picks up the vibrations of the sounds

around you, including your own voice. Be aware of what you say and how you say it, especially if you are with child.

The first sense to develop is that of hearing and it is the last to leave. Doctors can tell you that those revived from the near-death experience report that the last sense they were aware of was sound. Researchers will also tell you that certain

The Angel of Sound

studies of near-death experiences reveal that the most frequently experienced sound heard by people going through "the tunnel" to the other side was that of choral music ringing with vocal harmonics. From an interdimensional standpoint we can tell you that this is true. Vocal harmonics come as close to the singing of angels as you humans can create.

Listening

Hearing is an extraordinary sense—it really helps define reality. You can shut your eyes to block sight and breathe through your mouth to block smell, but it really is very difficult to block sound. Sound is all around us, and our sense of hearing aids in the creation of our reality. We would like to take this understanding one step further and remind you that hearing is a passive activity, because you often are not aware of the sounds that affect you. They could be vibrating your bodies and eardrums and triggering neuronal activity, but frequently you are unaware of them. Listening is a conscious activity. Through learning to listen we can heighten our consciousness and our awareness of reality.

An Exercise in Listening

Take a moment after you read this next paragraph. Close your eyes and listen to the sounds around you. What are you aware of? Listen as alertly as you can. Are you aware of the sounds of machines in your room or in a neighboring room? Or from the outside? Is there music playing? Birds calling? Is the wind blowing? Are there people talking nearby? Are

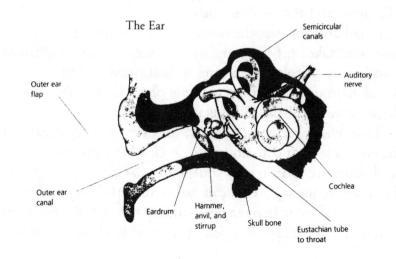

The Ear

Semicircular canals

Auditory nerve

Outer ear flap

Outer ear canal

Eardrum

Hammer, anvil, and stirrup

Skull bone

Cochlea

Eustachian tube to throat

there street sounds such as cars going by?

What are you listening to? Are you aware of the sound of your own breath or your heartbeat? Are you aware of the sound of the blood rushing through your veins or impulses moving through your nervous system? What are the sounds you are listening to? Take a moment and listen, and when you have finished note any differences you might have experienced before and after you listened. For many people the experience of active listening opens up new realms of sound.

Simply by learning to listen, we can dramatically heighten our perception of the world, thus altering our consciousness. Many meditation groups and spiritual paths use sound as a means of entering the divine. Listening to the *shabd,* the sound current, is an extraordinary yogic discipline. For many of these groups the inner sounds experienced by deep listening are among the most profound ways of traveling to higher planes. Some spiritual masters have even charted the sounds of different planes—from the sounds of bells ringing to the sounds of the ocean to the sounds of the humming of bees. Listening to inner sounds is very powerful indeed, as are the experiences of listening to outer sounds. And then there are harmonics, which might well be the bridge between the inner and the outer sounds.

Jonathan compares the new awareness harmonics to a person who takes off his sunglasses to see the true brightness and beauty of color. Learning to first listen and then create vocal harmonics is like removing plugs from your ears to become aware of the full spectrum of sound.

Thus vocal harmonics can be an extraordinary means of heightening your consciousness. It changes your brain waves and stimulates portions of your brain that can receive greater levels of frequency. This can be a wonderful way of beginning to shift your frequencies—simply through the power of listening. You begin to open up to new levels of sound and vibration through your ears, your mind and your heart.

On a physical level, different sounds affect brain waves, heartbeat and respiration differently. Some of these, such as the soothing sounds of the ocean or gentle music, can be very relaxing and therapeutic. Other sounds can actually stress the brain and body and have a negative effect on us. Listening to harmonically related sounds, particularly vocal music, can be one of the most uplifting and transformative experiences on this planet. It can relax and relieve stress and it can allow consciousness to travel to higher planes.

Important research indicates that by listening to sounds high in harmonics we can charge the brain and the body as well. Sounds rich in harmonics nourish the body, brain and psyche. Simply by listening to these sounds you can learn to shift your frequencies.

ⓦ   ⓦ   ⓦ

Chapter 6

Harmonics and the Brain

In chapter 5 we continued our discussion of vocal harmonics and delved into the importance of listening. We talked of the new vocal harmonic style that Jonathan calls nouveau-European vocal harmonics (to differentiate it from the different Eastern traditions) and how listening to these sounds can open the consciousness to new levels of awareness.

Listening

As we described last time, listening to vocal harmonics can create profound changes in consciousness. On a physiological level, merely listening to vocal harmonics can slow down one's heartbeat, respiration and brain waves, inducing deep states of relaxation. This by itself can be therapeutic and healing, since so much of the imbalance today is due to stress.

We also discussed the fact that listening to sounds rich in vocal harmonics can charge the cortex of the brain, providing an energy charge for the whole body. Such sounds can obviously stimulate and enhance the functions of the immune system.

This happens, you understand, as a result of simply *listening* to these sounds. It is not through the creation of vocal harmonics—that is a wholly different act, and the results are quite different and far more impressive. It is the difference between being a passive receiver of sound (by listening) and an active creator of sound. It is, as you say, like the difference between apples and oranges.

Self-Created Sound

Self-created sound affects you from inside out, whereas external sound affects you from outside in. There is really no comparison. Self-created sounds create a vibratory force—a resonance—within you that is difficult and frequently impossible to achieve through any other means. Different parts of the physical body, especially the brain, will resonate with the sound. Some like to say that self-created sound gives you an internal massage. While this is perhaps oversimplified, it is essentially correct—though of course much more than that happens.

The effect of resonance on the physical body and the associated chakras is a subject that we'll take up later. Vocal harmonics is an extraordinary means to shift frequency. As we have discussed before, using sound as a healing instrument is predicated on understanding that illness is a disharmony somewhere in the body. It is possible (and actually quite simple) to learn to use the voice to break up imbalanced patterns and restore the body's natural resonance.

The Brain

The brain is essentially a gelatinous glob encased within a hard, bony structure you call the cranium. Your scientists are struggling to understand and map the brain. They are having great success but at the same time great difficulty. A friend of Jonathan's once wrote a book on the brain and stated that the current scientific understanding is like this: If the brain were the size of the U.S., scientists so far have only succeeded in mapping the area from approximately New York to Philadel-

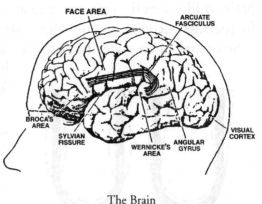

The Brain

phia. (Jonathan likes to say that the map merely goes from New York to Hoboken, New Jersey, but that is his own understanding and a bit of a joke at that.)

Scientists keep discovering new things about the brain and then finding further mysteries. One of the more baffling phenomena of the brain is that there are certain humans who, because of accident, disease or genetics, are born with brains that simply shouldn't function but do. Key portions of their brains are missing or damaged, but the people function normally. The humans who have these conditions don't know they can't, so they do. These are rare situations, of course, but they exist and serve to baffle biologists and surgeons. We wish to state that the brain is both a transmitter and receiver of high-frequency light-encoded information. Many of you know this.

The brain, that wonderful gelatinous glob, is very much undiscovered country, and will remain so, at least from your logical (dare we say left-brain?) point of view. Those examining the brain still see it merely as an organ that functions totally within the parameters of the physical body. In reality, the brain operates both inside *and* outside the body. It has a relationship to many different fields, frequencies and vibrational levels that can be perceived only esoterically. The brain is like a radio that can transmit and receive different frequencies, depending on which channel it is tuned to.

Scientists often state that only a small percentage of the brain is being used. This is true, for in order for humans to use the other portions of the brain, the trans-mitter/receiver must be tuned to different stations. There are many ways to change the frequency response of the brain, including meditation, light, nutrition, visualization, movement and, of course, sound. Sound might in fact be the easiest way of retuning the brain—which will in turn shift the frequencies of the entire vibratory field.

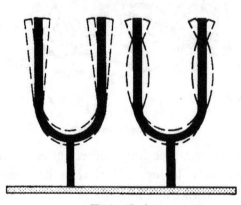

Tuning Forks

Stimulating the Brain with Sound

Within the realm of sound there are many different modalities for shifting the frequencies of the brain: through listening and through singing, chanting and toning. The most effective method Jonathan has found utilizes vocal har-monics, projecting specific harmonics to different portions of the brain. Electrical charges to the brain produce grosser effects than the acoustical resonance created by vocal har-monics.

The pituitary/pineal area is one of the major regulatory mechanisms for frequency response. By resonating this area with self-created sounds, all sorts of subsidiary resonant neural outlets are set into motion. This region is also associ-ated with the third eye and crown chakras.

There are many different subchakras within the head and brain, including the little-known alta major region at the back of the head near the occipital area. This region has been called the channeling chakra, because it is active during the channeling process.

Through use of intentionality coupled with specific vocal harmonics, various sites throughout the brain can be stimulated, causing the release of powerful neurochemicals such as melatonin and the endorphins (naturally created opiumlike substances) and other chemicals yet to be discovered. These sounds can create new brain connections, retune the brain and access higher levels of consciousness.

In the introduction to his book *Healing Sounds,* Jonathan discusses his experience in a temple in Palenque, Mexico. He was led to a totally dark underground room by a brujo who knew of Jonathan's work and understood what sound could do. Jonathan created and then projected vocal harmonics into the pineal, causing it to create melatonin. This unexpectedly created light—quite an amazing experience. (The pineal is a bioluminescent organ, meaning it has the ability to create light.) The sound Jonathan used, incidentally, is a sound he teaches in his workshops — the "nuuu-rrr" sound. Interestingly, this is an Eastern word for *light*. And it is a sound that, given the correct frequency and intention, we now know can create light.

We invite you to experiment with this sound and see what occurs. Please be aware that it is very difficult to see a word and then vocalize the sound that was intended—particularly when that sound is one that specifically generates harmonics. But we invite you to try.

In his book Jonathan suggests the possibility of creating new neural synapses in the brain, and that vocal harmonics might have great potential for treating humans with neurological brain disorders. Recently a scientist who read

Jonathan's work did research on one area and found that certain sounds did release melatonin. This scientist indicated that this might be therapeutic, perhaps in the treatment of cancer.

There is always the chance that someone will break away from the mainstream and begin actively investigating sound. Such an event might cause the medical community to sit up and take notice of sound's healing potential.

What does all this mean? That through sound we can help awaken ourselves to our full potential. We can get high; we can feel good. We can speak with spirits and guides. We can transmit and receive higher levels of vibrational energy. We can travel interdimensionally. We can do quite extraordinary things merely by making a sound with a specific intention.

It sounds simple, doesn't it? And it is.

ⓦ   ⓦ   ⓦ

Chapter 7

Energy Fields

In our previous conversation we continued our discussion of vocal harmonics and focused on the use of these sounds to change the tuning of the brain. As we said, the brain is an extraordinary instrument for receiving and transmitting frequencies that affect our body and etheric fields. We can also consciously influence other fields in the physical plane as well as other dimensions.

Energy Fields

Energy fields, whether physical, etheric or interdimensional, are constantly being created. It is only our awareness of them that is often deficient. Your scientists are beginning to understand their importance. There are all sorts of field theories being explored, and awareness of these fields is showing up in the cutting edge of medical and scientific research. It is important to recognize that etheric or subtle-energy fields have a role in forming the physical body and supplying energy to it. This kind of understanding has been handed down from the ancient practitioners of acupuncture. After having dismissed this healing art as a fraud for many years, the medical and scientific communities have awakened

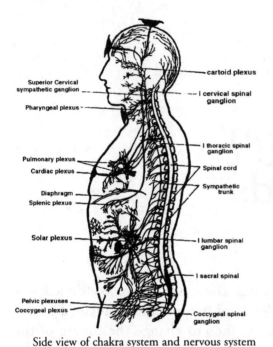

Superior Cervical
sympathetic ganglion

Pharyngeal plexus

cartoid plexus

l cervical spinal
ganglion

l thoracic spinal
ganglion

Pulmonary plexus

Cardiac plexus

Spinal cord

Sympathetic
trunk

Diaphragm
Splenic plexus

Solar plexus

l lumbar spinal
ganglion

l sacral spinal

Pelvic plexuses
Coccygeal plexus

Coccygeal spinal
ganglion

Side view of chakra system and nervous system

to the fact that no healing practice could survive for thousands of years were there no clear evidence that it worked. Humans have no patience for something that brings no results for that long—they are much too pragmatic. (Please do not tell us that you have put up with the various "nonworking" religions for an equal amount of time. We would answer that your religions do work for many—otherwise they would not be here.)

When your scientists finally decided to delve into the subject of acupuncture they discovered that there were electromagnetic points that could actually be measured with their seemingly primitive (from our viewpoint) instruments. Were they more sophisticated, they could measure far more aspects of subtle energy, including the chakras. The chakras remain a mystery to science, although anyone with any degree of heightened perception can experience them through sight, touch, or any of the other senses. However, the chakras will remain a mystery to science until a machine is invented that proves the existence of these spinning wheels of energy. (That, incidentally, is not too far away.)

We do not wish to denigrate your scientists, for they have done remarkable work. We merely suggest that there is an understanding of chakras from another level. Some of your scientists, having discovered the validity of acupuncture, are now exploring the realm of subtle energy. Through their limited equipment they have found that the acupuncture meridians of chicken embryos were formed before the actual organs, allowing some to wonder if the life field is created before the physical body is formed. In fact this is true.

Morphic Fields

Many of you know the term *morphic field*, which simply means "shape field"—a field that holds something in place. It can be something tangible like the physical body or something intangible like an energy vortex. Fields exist everywhere. They are created by movement, geometry, light—many different things.

Did you know that fields are even created whenever music is played? And did you know that one of the most effective ways for destroying a field is through harsh, percussive sounds? This knowledge, particularly the latter part, can assist those who want to break up thought forms, and it can help you understand some of the esoteric uses of rattles and drums in various shamanic traditions.

When musicians get together and play before an audience, they create a field (hopefully it is a beautiful and beneficial field, though sometimes it is not). What is the first thing the audience does? They clap. On one level this is an appreciation of the musicians, but on another level it almost immediately destroys the sonic field, as if the field were too intense for the audience to handle. Now, if you were truly aware of the field created by the sound, you would probably bathe in it, breathe it in and allow it to continue to affect your body and consciousness, because *it is in the silence after the sound that the truly transformative experiences occur. Most are not aware of these fields, so they destroy them in ignorance.*

It would take a major reeducation of your populations for

them to stop showing their appreciation through applause, and we do not suggest this just yet. We merely use this as an example of field awareness (or unawareness). As we stated, fields on your physical plane are continually created and uncreated (or destroyed), as are fields on the etheric and higher planes.

Fields are created by sound (which is our focus) as well as other wave forms. Electricity is one of your commonest forms of generating fields, and many of you are sensitive to those fields. Magnetism and microwaves are other sources. Light can also create fields, as do crystals and sacred geometry. Many of you can sense the fields created through artwork such as paintings and sculptures. Movement also creates fields, including that of your own body. Then there are the fields created by thought forms.

Electromagnetic Fields

Electrically generated fields have now come to the attention of your scientists, as have those fields generated by magnetic currents. Your scientists have known about these fields for many years, but their effects have only recently reached public awareness. For the scientists and their funding sources it was simply a matter of denial. Research by some awakened beings would show that fields generated by high-voltage power lines cause stress directly related to proximity and energy level, which in turn cause disease and damage, especially to young children and fetuses. Research disclosing the effects of these electric fields has been covered up and deceitful research publicized. The openness of these times has allowed this information to reach the public after many years, though little change has yet occurred.

We do not wish to imply that *all* fields generated by electric and other sources are inevitably hazardous to biological health. It is possible to create a field that actually enhances life energy. However, these are very specifically created fields, not haphazardly generated as the result of supplying some other need, as is the case with your power lines.

The biosystem creates its own field through electromagnetism, sound, light and other energy. In the three-dimensional world this begins at a subatomic level, with electrons revolving around the nucleus of an atom. We are on one level simply atoms vibrating together, and these atoms create fields of electricity, magnetism, sound and light, which become more coherent and immense until, for example, we look at the human biological system, which is a complex field generator.

In a healthy human these naturally created fields all work together. They are harmonically related and in balance. However, this field is relatively weak, and when it comes in contact with technologically created fields, it is often influenced by that externally created field, sometimes to such a degree that the latter is able to encode itself into the natural field, causing chaos within the biosystem.

Brainwaves

The electrical activities within the human brain are easily measurable by your EEG instrumentation, and these activities create a field. The brain pulses and vibrates with our breathing and heartbeat and thinking processes, all of them at different rates. It is interesting to note that brain waves are measured like sound, in cycles per second,

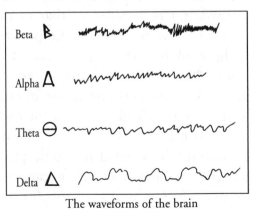

The waveforms of the brain

or Hertz (Hz). Brain waves are categorized by the four levels of consciousness they accompany: (1) beta: 12 to 25 Hz, normal waking activity; (2) alpha: 8 to 12 Hz, light meditation and daydreaming; (3) theta: 4 to 8 Hz, deeper meditation, shamanic work and deep active sleep; and (4) delta: .5 to 4 Hz, deepest meditation, shamanic work, channeling and deep passive sleep. The slower the brain waves, the deeper the state of relaxation and consciousness.

Brain waves are easily influenced by external stimuli, including electromagnetism and sound. If the biosystem enters a strong field specifically calibrated to affect the brain, the brain can be affected in a matter of seconds. A calm and relaxed person might enter one of these fields and within moments begin to feel tense and agitated. The individual is not, of course, aware he has entered such a field, but the biosystem nevertheless responds. Some sensitive individuals are aware of these responses, yet they are usually unable to do anything about it.

Computers generate fields, as do your television sets and electric lights. Sonic technologies such as stereos and natural and unnatural sounds of humans and their machines create their own fields. Noise pollution from jets, trains, traffic, heavy machinery and other sources has been a major contributor to imbalances that manifest as disease. Unless you can move to a mountaintop away from the technologies of humankind (which is no guarantee of escaping fields generated by satellites, microwave antennas, jet planes and so on), your jobs and homes are in environments that expose you to myriad fields. That is the bad news.

What is one to do? Most humans live in a seething pool of frequencies created for some purpose unrelated to reinforcing the biosystem. How can one live a healthful life in spite of this? The title of this forum is *Shifting Frequencies*, and its focus is teaching how to use our own self-created sounds to vibrate in harmony with the fields we experience. That is the good news. While we are constantly experiencing these fields, it is possible to learn to use the voice and, by combining our frequencies with our intent, generate a field that is not disturbed by externals. Here is an illustrative experience.

An Experience in Changing Fields

Sometimes when Jonathan teaches he finds himself in environments not necessarily conducive to the experiences he wishes to create. When this happens he works with them, for he is grateful for the opportunity to share. At one particular workshop he experienced a most challenging environment. The room in which he would teach was beautiful, with marble floors, walls and a ceiling that would reinforce the sonics made by the group. But there was an already existing field there; a very loud hum or buzz generated by some electric or magnetic system was being amplified by the room's wonderful acoustics. It was so loud that it actually drowned out the lower frequencies of Jonathan's voice when he spoke. Even more challenging, it created a field that made everyone in the room jittery and nervous.

After five minutes Jonathan realized it could not be ignored; it was too enormous and powerful. There was no place to move the workshop, so Jonathan and the group had to put up with it. The question was, how? "Let's tone with this sound and see what happens," Jonathan suggested. "Maybe we can turn an adversary into an ally." Jonathan and the group matched the pitch of the sound and toned with it for about twenty minutes. It really was quite lovely. After that the sound was quieter and less distracting and the effects of the field were less disturbing. What had happened in this case was that rather than fight the frequency, they simply shifted their own frequencies to attune with the field that was being generated. Their nervous systems no longer battled the frequency, but resonated with it instead. The reattunement was so powerful that many in the group began to find the sound soothing, like the low *om* of a Tibetan monk.

A few students had entered the room during the toning experience and then heard the sound when the group ceased toning. These students thought that the low-frequency hum was actually a recording playing softly in the background, designed to help induce peace and calm. During a break one of them asked Jonathan if she could purchase this recording. It was, in retrospect, quite humorous, and became a marvelous opportunity for Jonathan to share his work with shifting frequencies. We are glad to report it was a success.

While we do not recommend this sort of experience if it can be avoided, consider the possibility that you can work with a field that you encounter. You can learn to use your own sounds to shift your own frequencies, and when you encounter inharmonious fields, you can temporarily shift your own field and be at peace and in health. And yes, you can shift it back at any time, as Jonathan and his students did.

🜂　　🜂　　🜂

Chapter 8

Creating
Sacred Space

In previous chapters we began exploring the concepts of energy fields and their relationship with
frequency-shifting. We discussed the idea that
energy fields are created constantly — through electromagnetism, sound, light and thought, to name a few. And
because we encounter these fields so consistently, we are constantly being affected by them. We ended the chapter by
stating that sound could be used to help us adjust to these
different fields we encounter. We would like to speak more
about fields.

Human Fields

The discovery that human beings themselves create energy
fields is not new. How could it be, when your ancient mystics were aware of them? They called them chakras and subtle bodies and gave them all sorts of interesting names. In
the early part of this century the fields created by one aspect
of the electromagnetic spectrum were discovered by a professor at one of your major universities. He proved conclu-
sively that humans had electromagnetic fields —from the
fields created by the individual cells to that of the entire

human biosystem. He also showed that the fields created by
disease were disharmonious with the rest of the biosystem.

Many of you are not aware of this researcher's work
because when this once-esteemed professor attempted to
publish material on his discovery, he was shunned and
scorned by his colleagues. His work was never publicized; it
was essentially ignored. Now, more than fifty years later, his
work is beginning to be acknowledged. Have you noticed
that frequently when advanced discoveries are made that do
not fit the current dogmas, those discoveries are dormant
until the rest of the world has caught up? This has also happened with many spiritual leaders and their teachings. No
doubt some of you reading this feel out of sync with the rest
of the world and find this challenging. It is understandable
if your thinking and consciousness go beyond that of the
mainstream, but thankfully, frequencies are shifting now.
There is a tremendous escalation of consciousness, so it will
not be quite so challenging or lonely anymore.

Creating Fields

Energy fields and their effects seem to dictate the form of
your universe, yet most are unaware of this. Over a dozen
years ago Jonathan was shown how to dowse at a workshop.
At one point the instructor had the class create an invisible
wall with thought while he was in the next room. His students, trying to be clever, created an invisible zig-zag wall.
Yet this dowser was able to determine exactly where the wall
with its zigs and zags had been created. The field created by
the thought forms was powerful enough to be detected by
dowsing. It made Jonathan aware that events created fields,
and that these fields were detectable by those who were sensitive to them—even those that occurred lifetimes ago.

One could, for example, walk into a room where a certain
action had taken place and, if one were conscious enough,

actually experience that action from an earlier time. Psychics and sensitives do this frequently. The thought forms around actions and events create fields that can last a very long time. If these actions and events take place in a sacred manner, they begin to build on each other, creating a marvelous energy. One explanation for why certain power spots remain power spots is that sacred acts took place frequently there and still continue somehow, amplifying the already-existing energy fields initially created there.

Power Spots

We are not suggesting that your so-called power spots are powerful simply because sacred acts have taken place there. It is common knowledge that many places of power were used and built upon by the ancients because they were located at or near Earth grid lines and fields of energy. Sacred activity at those power spots will "amp up" that energy even further. Still further energy amplification can be created through the use of sacred geometries. The structure of the pyramids are an example of this, as are many cathedrals in Europe.

Sound is an extremely powerful tool for creating sacred space. Those of you who have made sounds in these sacred power spots know this. When you have sounded in spaces that are *not* considered power spots you also know you can create a field yourself. Almost anyplace can become a sacred space and power spot if the individuals present use the formula of *vocalization + visualization = manifestation* to create the field. This is particularly true if individuals continue to hold the field they have created and do not allow it to be corrupted by other fields.

Sacred Sounds

If, for example, one goes into a wooded area (sacred by its

The scared Hindu syllable 'Om,' when correctly uttered into the tonoscope, apparently produces the circle 'O,' which is then filled in with concentric squares and triangles, finally producing, when the last traces of the 'm' have dies away, a 'yantra'—the formal geometrical expression of scared vibration which is found in many of the world's religions.

very being, since nature is sacred) with a group and then does sacred chanting, perhaps invoking some divine being, then that area will resonate with the energy of the invoked being. Its energy will continue to manifest, particularly if the area is turned into a temple, with offerings made to it. However, if it were turned into a target range or something equally offensive, the energy would likely be corrupted.

Sound builds upon itself; this is especially true of sacred sound. A sacred sound that has been activated through constant chanting is charged and particularly powerful. Let us use *om* as an example. At any given moment on Earth there are doubtless many people engaged in chanting the *om*. Now, that is a very powerful sound indeed and also very popular. The field it creates resonates all the time because it is being chanted somewhere all the time. Thus it is easy to tap into its power and resonate with its energy.

It would be more difficult to activate an ancient Babylonian mantra that had not been used for many thousands of years, because that ancient mantra and the divine energy and beings associated with it have been dormant so long. They must be awakened. That is not difficult to do, but it does take conscious direction and an understanding of the energies being created.

Certain sacred words in various languages have lost much of their power because they are no longer chanted with sacred intention. These mantras have simply become words that are usually translated as "hello" or "good-bye" or "peace." Your *om*, in fact, is very much like this, for one of its meanings is "peace." Besides being used in speech to convey meaning, it is also chanted in a sacred manner. For that reason, *om* has maintained its sacred energy field. The true power of words such as the Hebrew "shalom" or the Hawaiian "aloha" as mantras (we use these two only as examples, for there are many more such words) has been lessened because they are no longer being used as sacred sounds. They can be activated with sacred intent and with visualization — remember the formula: *vocalization + visualization = manifestation?* This is not to say that your rabbis and kahunas have not continued to use *shalom* and *aloha* in a sacred manner, but that their sacredness has been forgotten by the majority of the people who use those words.

Jonathan has had the experience of chanting both "shalom" and "aloha" in elongated fashion (each chant of the word taking an entire breath) with large groups of people. Before they began to chant, he had these groups focus upon the meaning of the words, their intent while sounding them, and specific visualizations they encoded on them. The effect of chanting these words was truly marvelous. All sorts of white light and feelings of love manifested, and people felt divine energies surging through the group. These were words that both groups had used on a daily basis, but never before in such a manner. They were able to reactivate the fields earlier created by these words through working with intent and visualization and by acknowledging these words again as sacred sounds.

The aspect of energy fields created by sound is one of the reasons why the formula *vocalization + visualization = man-*

ifestation is so powerful. It is basically the encoding of a thought form upon a sound. And if this sonically encoded thought form already exists (such as with the *om* or *shalom* or *aloha*), it is easy to activate it and resonate with it. You can then create sacred fields with those sounds. This is good news for those of you who want to change the vibrational frequency of different places. Simply find a chant and the appropriate energy (or deity) that you like. Then create the sacred sound by using sacred intent and visualization.

Om, shalom and *aloha* are excellent sounds for this. (There are, of course, countless others, depending upon your culture and tradition.) These three sounds all work with a similar wave form of love and peace. They are usually not associated with specific deities, but with the specific energies of light and love, peace and harmony. They are, however, excellent for creating and activating sacred space and for changing the vibrational frequencies of areas that need it.

Working with specific mantras that invoke specific energies and also with specific deities or beings is a good way to start. Invoking beings who represent aspects of compassion is particularly helpful. Many beings are joyous to be of assistance to those on Earth — Tara, Christ, Kuan Yin and Avalokitesvara are but a few of them.

Tara
The Victorious Usnisa of Tathagatas

These beings are similar, for they represent the wave form of compassion. This wave form has been anthropomorphized in many different traditions, thus you have many different names for beings who represent compassion. Some are male, some female, but they are found in every religious tradition and spiritual path. They have similar qualities and attributes, the most basic being that of helping instill the essence of compassion in the invoker.

⦿   ⦿   ⦿

Chapter 9

Compassion Through Sound

L ast chapter we concluded our current discussion on fields and focused on using sound to create and influence fields. We began and will continue today discussing the invocation of energy forms of compassion to activate and resonate with these sacred spaces.

Love and Fear

It is said that there are only two basic emotions: love and fear. There is much truth to this. Out of the energies of love come many other emotions, such as joy, ecstasy and happiness. Out of the energies of fear come other emotions, such as anger, despair and hatred. This, of course, is an oversimplification, but you get the idea. It is important to understand that our lives and the reality we create are filtered through emotion and that we tend to see things through a prism of either love or fear.

It has been suggested that to reach higher dimensions of consciousness, one must be in a state of love. When talking about higher dimensionalities, the idea of a fourth or fifth dimension is often brought up. Recently a friend of Jonathan's came back from a conference, saying, "I was in the fifth dimension." After being asked what that was, the friend replied, "You know, when everything is happening just right and you're in the flow, when everything is synchronistic and things you think about occur immediately."

We like this simple definition that describes a state where thoughts become reality. Jonathan believes that if that is truly the fifth dimension, we might already have entered it. There is truth to this, for your thoughts do create reality. However, the realities you create for yourself are not necessarily the kindest, the gentlest, the most loving. Many times these realities arise and are created through fear. If Jonathan's friend was operating from the fifth dimension (or whatever you want to call it), that was a frequency based in love, not fear. Jonathan suggested this to his friend, adding that perhaps when he resumed his normal everyday life, he might again operate out of fear. The friend agreed.

Clearing the emotional body is of great importance in these amazing, transformative times. If you are becoming more and more capable and conscious of cocreating your realities, you can observe both the negative and the positive aspects of your creations come into being. Any concern you might have is addressed by the mystics and spiritual messengers who throughout time, have always said that *love is the answer*.

This book is about shifting frequencies, particularly about ways that sound can be utilized to create vibrational change. Yet we tell you that the greatest frequency shift that can ever occur is when one shifts from fear to love. This is the most extraordinary vibrational change one can experience. And yes, sound can be a wonderful vehicle for doing this.

Love As a Wave

Love is a vibration. It has been postulated that love is a long, coherent wave form that actually interfaces with the

DNA helixes, thereby encoding and then running that program and shifting the frequency. On the other hand, fear has been postulated to be a short, incoherent wave form that creates the opposite effect on DNA. Experiments were done in a laboratory not long ago in which a DNA strand was unbraided. Then a group of researchers, working solely with the vibration of love as a thought form, gathered around this unbraided DNA and beamed love at it, whereupon the DNA recoiled itself. What an extraordinary experiment and what a remarkable result!

We do not, by the way, suggest that the wave form of love or fear can be reduced to mere frequency in terms of measurement via cycles per second. This is an oversimplification. Long waves of frequency are not more "loving" than short waves. (Otherwise bass notes would be more loving than treble notes, and they are not.) In terms of feelings, however, when you are in a loving state it is undeniable that you are in a much different vibrational state than when you are in fear. And when you are in a loving state, your heartbeat, respiration and brain waves are very different from your fearful state. In love your brain waves are slow, as is your heartbeat and respiration. In a fearful state your brain waves are rapid, as is your heartbeat and respiration. These are *effects* of the frequencies of love and fear and cannot be reduced to cycles per second of sound.

The "Ah" Sound

Sound can, however, help trigger the response of love. If you would like to try this exercise, sit quietly for a few moments and think of a very loving experience you have had. As you think of this experience, begin to sound forth a very gentle "ah." Make this sound long and extended: "Aaaaaahhhhhh . . ." and while you do this with the thought or intention of love, feel your heart chakra resonate with it.

Feel your heart center opening, balancing and aligning with this energy. The *ah* sound is an excellent sound for working with the energy of the heart center and the feeling of love. It is the sound Jonathan uses to resonate the heart center when he leads workshops in an exercise he calls Vowels as Mantras. There are different sounds for different chakras, but the *ah* sound seems to work nicely for the heart.

The *ah* sound is also found in many of the god and goddess names on the planet—Krishn*a*, Buddh*a*, Yeshu*a* (Jesus), Av*a*lokitesv*a*r*a*, *A*ll*a*h, W*a*k*a*ntank*a*, Y*a*hW*a*y, Apollo, T*a*r*a*, Athen*a*, S*a*r*a*sw*a*ti, G*a*i*a*, Shekin*a*, to name a few. Do you think this is coincidence? Of course not.

The *ah* sound, of course, is only one of many sounds that conveys the energy of love. We bring it to your attention as a simple sound you can work with. And it does not resonate only with the heart chakra; all of your chakras can and will someday resonate to the energy of love as you use many sounds to convey that energy. *All sounds* can in fact resonate with the energy of love. When this time comes, all sounds will be sacred sounds, for you will have reached a point in your development where the intention of the sound supersedes its frequency. Then you will have reached a point in your consciousness where you can truly resonate with the energy of what Jonathan's friend called the fifth dimension.

Compassion

Compassion is a key to working with the energy of love, for compassion is the understanding of the *unconditional energy* of love. Unconditional love—what a wonderful concept to conceive, and what a difficult concept to achieve! To love unconditionally is to love each and every being as sacred. How extraordinary and how challenging, for to love in this manner is to break down the separation between you and realize the oneness of all life. It is not an easy thing.

Perhaps the gentlest way to experience this unconditional love is to start with oneself. If you have already forgiven yourself for whatever imperfections you might have experienced as a human, then you might be able to begin loving others unconditionally (we do not mean only humans, but all life). The key to unconditional love initially lies in loving oneself. When you can truly love yourself without condition (for otherwise it would not be unconditional), then you are ready to move toward

The Bodhisattva Avalokitesvara of the renowned mantra Om-Mani-Padme-Hum.

truly loving others. Even divine entities can have difficulty here.

The Avalokitesvara

In the Buddhist tradition there is a being known as the Avalokitesvara, the bodhisattva of compassion, whose name has been translated as "sound that illuminates the world." This being reached enlightenment in the physical, but instead of traveling to the highest of heavenly realms to receive his just rewards, the Avalokitesvara decided to stay and help out on the Earth and other planes until all sentient beings reached enlightenment. Legend has it that after only a short time the Avalokitesvara became so despondent over all the suffering in the world that he blew apart from the pain. Another divine entity, his spiritual father, came to the Avalokitesvara's aid, putting him back together and giving counsel and increased abilities. The Avalokitesvara realized that even if he helped only one other being, he was doing extraordinary work.

We tell this story to emphasize what an extraordinary gift that compassion is and how difficult to embody. With compassion comes the awareness of all the fear on the planet and the resulting suffering. It is an incredibly loving state, but one that might be accompanied by sadness until one is able to detach from the limited self. Then one can realize what a gift compassion is—to love unconditionally despite all the fear from others that one encounters. As one comes into the consciousness of compassion, it is important to realize that through assistance from the divine, as the Avalokitesvara learned, all is possible.

Compassion is necessary for those who work with the energy of healing. With compassion you empathize and resonate with others until they become as one with you, and the fears and imbalances become transmuted through the energy of love. Healing occurs through this perfect oneness. It is with this passion that you transmit the energies of healing, whether they be through sound, light, touch or whatever.

We briefly discussed last time how the Christ and many others have embodied the wave form of compassion, and that this wave form could create sacred space and shift the frequencies of self and others. Working with this energy through sounding is truly awe-inspiring.

Once Jonathan had a student who was very interested in

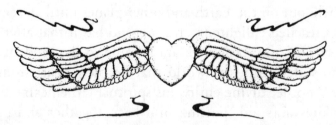

Winged Heart

finding the right frequency for diffusing negative energy. Jonathan told the student that he did not feel there was one correct frequency for this, but that projecting sound with the simple intention of love might be quite effective for remedying this situation. Jonathan also suggested that the student work with specific mantras that utilized this energy—particularly the Om Mani Padme Hum chant (the mantra that invokes the Avalokitesvara) and others the student felt comfortable with.

The next day the student reported that he was driving home when he saw a car driving erratically. Concerned that this car would cause an accident, he began a mantric chant while projecting the energy of love. The other car (with a student driver) suddenly stopped the driving practice. During the rest of the two-hour drive home the student continued the mantric chanting, beaming love at dangerous or aggressive drivers—and it worked. We like to believe that the student was in the so-called fifth dimension during that time. We are grateful for all who are in that state.

Sounding with the energy of compassion, whether through mantric chanting, vowel sounds or other sacred sounds, is extraordinary when done alone, although it is even better when done in a group. This is not said to downplay the effect of individual sounding, but to stress the extraordinary effect that group sounding accomplishes. In groups the consciousness that can be achieved is virtually unimaginable.

Sacred Sound in a Group

Sound and intentionality build upon each other synergistically. When Jesus said he would be around when two or more were gathered in his name, he was not speaking figuratively. The effect of sacred sound in a group is like that. The mathematics are very different: one plus one equal three—or even more.

So we suggest again to you to gather together in sacred sound and experience the results. You can create sacred space in this manner. You can change the frequencies of imbalanced areas in this way. And the energy will stay changed, at least for a while, because you have charged the fields with sacred sound. All who enter that field will themselves be affected and changed, long after your own sounds have died away.

Remember when sounding together in a group to have a common intention. We suggest that one of the intentions might be to become channels of divine light and love using sacred sound. If you can add visualization to the sound, either by invoking specific entities who work with love or by seeing the sound manifesting sacred geometries of love, this will amplify and focus the energy you are working with. Working with sound in this manner, you will be assisting not only your personal frequency shifts and of those around you, but the frequency shifts of the planet itself.

⦿　　⦿　　⦿

Chapter 10

Sacred Geometry and Sound

We would like to begin a discussion of sacred geometry or, more particularly, the relationship between sound and sacred geometry. This is a topic that seems to resonate with many of you, quite understandably. Sacred geometry is one of the building blocks of reality. Many of you are intrigued by the concept of sacred geometry and how it relates to the physical and the higher planes.

Before we begin we would like to discuss what is meant by "reality." What is it? In a sense, both everything and nothing is reality. All is subject to change. What you perceive as reality at any given moment might suddenly shift to something that is far different. Reality is fluid, constantly altering itself, depending on the thought forms you create.

The Great Mystery

There is a current belief that sacred geometry is the foundation of reality—that the construction and creation of the universe is based on sacred geometry. On one level, this is true. However, on another level this is another attempt to understand and explain what is unexplainable. The struc-

ture of the universe—indeed, the machinations of the cosmos—have frequently been called by the different sages
through time the Great Mystery. Now, however, this Great
Mystery is being explained by some through the concepts of
sacred geometry. While sacred geometry is an important
part of the understanding of life, the universe and everything
(as one writer called it), it is by no means the complete picture.

Throughout the ages there have been those who have
sought to explain the Great Mystery through various means.
Some used sounds, others used symbols and still others,
words—it does not matter. They were all worthy attempts
to explain the unexplainable, and as such simply become
(from our perspective) other limited concepts that offer the
mind-intriguing possibilities for understanding. Humans
(and beings from other dimensions, galaxies and whatnot), if
they desire to know the unknowable, will resort to create systems and boxes within which to put those systems so they
can feel secure about knowing the unknowable.

The unknowable is just that—unknowable. You can grasp
glimpses of it, but much like your parable of the blind men
feeling the elephant, each person touches a different part.
One feels the trunk and says, "The elephant is like a vine."
Another feels the leg and says, "The elephant is like a tree."
Another feels the body and says, "The elephant is like a
rock." Another feels the tail and says, "The elephant is like
a snake," and so on. Each limited perception is true from
that perspective and that person's reality. Yet none of them
are wholly correct about what an *elephant* is. So it is with the
universe and sacred geometry.

If you were to view reality constructs from our perspective,
you would understand that there are countless planes within
planes—untold dimensions, limitless levels of consciousness.
And each of these planes is based on the beliefs and thought

forms of those who created them. Thus, like the blind men feeling the elephant, each of these planes is real and correct within that limited context, yet none of them are the big picture. There are, for example, planes in which different geometric forms comprise the reality construct. Those who tap into these planes will try to tell you that this is the basis of the universe. Yet there are also planes in which archetypes are the governing structures. Those who resonate to these constructs will tell you that archetypes are really the basis of reality. All are true, and none are true, depending on your chosen context. But the big picture—the Great Mystery—is beyond the comprehension of mortals and immortals. You can get part of the picture, but only part. Believe us when we tell you this, and take great joy in it, because the Great Mystery is not meant to be fully understood. It is an illusion to think it can, yet it is great fun trying.

This is not to suggest that you should not begin to explore your own divinity and the divinity of all. We urge you to do so; continue to develop your divine consciousness. This is all part of the plan—the evolutionary steps you are taking to become greater than you are. But do not assume that any one step of evolution

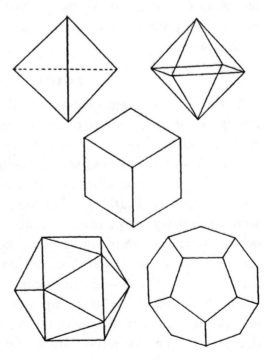

Platonic Solids

and enlightenment contains the answer to the way things are for all beings.

It has been said that the Way that can be told is not the Way. We agree. We urge you to explore, for that is necessary, but do not be fooled into believing you have found "it." The "it" that you have found has always been around in one form or another, and different entities on different planets have always fallen into the trap of believing they have found "it." Reality is fluid, and the "it" will always change. Even though we urge you to explore finding "it," we also urge you to avoid the belief that you have found "it" and can stop the process of growth your search has brought you.

We have gone to rather elaborate lengths to tell you this because there seem to be so many people who believe that sacred geometry is the "it" that will fully explain the Way, the big picture, the Great Mystery. While it does explain a worthwhile portion, it is only a portion. We applaud the exploration.

Form

At the core of sacred geometry is the understanding that one aspect of the structure of the universe is based on form. And that within this form-based universe are simple shapes. This understanding is simple and obvious, not really mysterious. What is astounding is that it has been forgotten by your current civilization. Through your rediscovery of sacred geometry, extraordinary shifts in consciousness will occur. Certainly your ancient civilizations had an understanding and an awareness of sacred geometry and how geometric forms were found throughout the universe. Some claim that through appreciating sacred geometry one can unlock the secrets of the ancients. We would like to suggest that your ancients (whether Greeks, Egyptians or earlier cultures in and before your recorded history) did not have the big picture, either. They had extraordinary secrets worthy of rediscovery, but they did not have them all. Otherwise they would not have perished beneath the ocean waves or the desert sands.

Numbers and Shapes

Knowledge of sacred geometry begins with numbers and an understanding of the harmony inherent in the numbers and the shapes they create. Sacred geometric forms have, in fact, been called the archetypes of numbers, and at one level this is true. Different qualities have been attributed to different numbers and their inherent forms.

The number 1, the **monad**, represents the circle, within which all other forms can be housed. The number 2, the duality, can be seen as two overlapping circles, which creates within itself the vesica pisces, from which all other forms can manifest. The trinity—3—is represented by the equal-sided or equilateral triangle. The number 4 begets the square. The number 5 creates the pentagon. The number 6 is manifest as the hexagon and so on. Each shape unfolds and evolves to create another shape, another form. These shapes are found throughout the sacred architecture of your planet, and the qualities inherent in them seem to be essentially agreed upon by the mystics of different traditions. The qualities and attributes of the numbers and their geometries is too vast a subject to cover here, but there are numerous books and teachers on the subject.

What is most wondrous is that these shapes are found throughout nature. They can be created through sound— the divine sound of the Great Mystery. Some years ago one of your scientists created experiments that showed that powdered plastics, pastes, liquids, pollen and sand, when exposed to different sound frequencies, take on extraordinary geometric forms. He believed that these forms related to the harmonic sounds. Many years before, Goethe once said, "Architecture is frozen music," and we would agree.

Sound embodies both sacred geometry and numbers. Another scientist, truly enchanted by the phenomena of sound harmonics and numbers, believed that through harmonics the qualities of numbers could be appreciated, along with their quantitative effects.

Take a walk and look at the trees and other wonders of nature and you will find sacred geometry in abundance. Just by observing nature, one can begin to receive an appreciation of the numbers and the qualities inherent in that geometry. Nature manifests as divine creational form, an aspect of the Great Mystery. Yet numbers, like geometry, are only one aspect of the divine Creator's form. The same is true for sound. Do not believe that the universe breaks down into numbers *as we know them,* for in certain dimensions one plus one equals three. There are planes upon planes, realities upon realities, and their laws and constructs would differ, depending on where you are.

The newfound interest in sacred geometry is bringing some of the mysteries of the ancients into our modern ideology, enhancing our current evolution. Perhaps the greatest thing achieved by this new interest in sacred geometry is the activation of portions of the brain and psyche that have long been dormant.

Visualization

To truly understand and work with geometric forms, it is necessary to visualize these forms. Try this for yourself: Visualize an equal-sided triangle. (If you have difficulty, look at a drawing of an equilateral triangle for a minute or two, then close your eyes and see it against your eyelids.)

Next transform this two-dimensional triangle into a three-dimensional tetrahedron (three-sided pyramid). Now let it revolve so that you can view it from different angles and sides. These exercises are just the beginning of sacred geometry work, but this gives you an idea of the process.

When you visualize a geometric form, it is always accompanied by the field generated by that form. Creating a three-dimensional model will do it, too. These fields, whether created by visualization or by a model, exist at different vibratory levels, starting with the astral.

Mandalas

In Tibet and within many other magical traditions, visualizing is a sacred science. Tibetan monks spend much time visualizing a specific kind of geometric form that can be infinitely varied, called *mandalas*. They consciously create these thought forms and build further upon them. Mandalas literally exist on other planes of consciousness. After they build these mandalas in their meditations, they actually travel to the planes where these forms exist. These mandalas have their dimensional constructs as well as fields of energy. These meditations require much discipline; however, the results are extraordinary.

Mandalas utilize sacred geometric forms in their construction. Many of them also work with entities specific to a tradition. The Tibetans, for example, might have over 100 gods and goddesses housed in particular locations of the form they are mentally constructing.

Many who work with sacred geometry have similar activities and some even teach others how to use specific geometric forms as vehicles for traveling through the different planes. We will discuss these "merkabahs" later.

Constructing and using sacred geometric forms is, in principle, similar to the Tibetans' work with mandalas. One difference is that visualizing geometric forms does not require a particular belief system; it is quite nonsectarian. Anyone can play the game without feeling they are betraying their spiritual path. One does not need to worship Buddha, for example, in order to visualize a tetrahedron and travel in it to different dimensions.

Geometric forms used in this manner can be a powerful and effective tool for expanding consciousness. It is simpler and quicker than the extraordinary discipline needed for mandala work. Sometimes results can be achieved in hours, days, weeks or months, rather than the many years required for traditional mandala construction. Although you can't expect to gain instant enlightenment, visualizing and using geometric forms serves as a wonderful tool for accelerated evolution.

In addition to creating fields and using geometric forms to travel, there is yet another activation that occurs through working with sacred geometry. During visualization, portions of the mind/brain are used in a manner that many people might not have experienced in this lifetime. Visualizing geometric figures is a higher evolutionary function that stimulates the mind/brain most wondrously. New connections are made in the brain, allowing people to develop tier consciousness. Visualization—particularly visualization through sacred geometry—is a key (though not the only one) to the leap to frequency-shifting and accessing fifth-dimensional (and higher) consciousness. We applaud all of you who are working with this wonderful tool for frequency-shifting.

Next chapter we will focus on relationships between sound and geometry and in particular on the travel vehicles you call merkabahs.

ⓦ   ⓦ   ⓦ

Chapter 11

Merkabahs

L ast chapter we began a discussion of sacred geometry. We noted that there were many planes of consciousness and that encompassing geometric forms were among them. The interest in sacred geometry is beginning to expand (dare we joke and say geometrically) as beings continue on their evolutionary passage.

Understanding and use of sacred geometry allows you to access some of the ancient mysteries. It also enables you to tap into part of your psyche that enables you to access deeper realms of consciousness. It is a very valuable tool.

Sound and Sacred Geometry

Sound creates form, and thus sound is sacred geometry and vice versa. It is that simple. When coupled with specific visualizations, harmonically related sounds enable you to create fields of sacred geometry that are much stronger and more present than those created merely through visualization. The addition of sound with the visualization creates a third-dimensionality (or physicality) to the field, as well as enhancing higher-dimensional aspects of the field.

Sacred geometry can also be understood as numbers and

ratios. As we have previously discussed, sound and particularly harmonics, can also be understood in terms of numbers and ratios. The Pythagorean triangle, for example, expresses ratios (at times) of 3 to 4 to 5. This triangle, which can be used as a building block for many different geometric forms, can also be expressed sonically through specific harmonics. For example, in the keynote that you call "C," this 3-4-5 ratio can be expressed as the notes G, C and E, which creates a particular inversion of what is called a *major triad.* In the above case, this chord is C major. Through sounding these notes as intervals and harmonics, it is quite easy to create a Pythagorean triangle and use this triangle to build other forms.

The shaded figure is the star tetrahedron of the merkabah

The above information expresses an important key to understanding a relationship between sound and sacred geometry and how the two can be used together. Jonathan deals with this material in a much more detailed and comprehensive fashion in the higher levels of his teachings.

Some years ago Jonathan was guided to begin creating what he called "interdimensional" fields that he would create with the higher level groups he was training. This field was a specific geometric form that was created through the process of group sounding and visualization. Do you remember the formula: *Vocalization + Visualization = Manifestation?* Using particular intervals, harmonics, colors and geometries, Jonathan and the groups created an energy field that could be utilized to travel to different realities or to bring other dimensional energies to his group.

Jonathan had been working intuitively during his initial experience with the creation of this field. Of course he was being given much guidance by us, but we left the outcome as a surprise. What Jonathan discovered was that by using sound, color, geometry and intention, he was able to manifest a form that was tangible on the third-dimensional level. It could be felt by members of the group and seen by some. It displayed a unique gravitational

By placing the four letters of the tetragrammaton in a vertical column a figure resembling a human form is produced, the first He the arms and shoulders, the Vau the trunk of the body, and the last He the hips and legs. Even if the Hebrew letters are exchanged for their English equivalents, the form is not dramatically altered.

field, as well as time/space aspects. After this form was created, the group moved the form up to the skies and into the earth to act as a frequency-shifting tool for the planet. Since then, a number of such forms have been created, linking together for planetary acceleration.

What was that form? It was a diamond-shaped, wondrous object that pulsed and oscillated in many directions and dimensionalities. At the time, Jonathan simply called it an interdimensional field. Since then, a term has come into your common vernacular that nicely describes this field — *merkabah*.

Merkabah

Merkabah is an ancient Hebrew word that means "chariot." This comes from Ezekiel's encounter in the Old Testament. The term merkabah (spelled many ways in the English language) has been used by students of the Kabbalah for many centuries to mean a vehicle with which to travel to the different planes (or emanations) of God (the ten sephiroth of the Tree of Life). Most recently it has come into usage as meaning a specific geometric form called a star tetrahedron, with which individuals can travel to higher dimensions.

Those of you who are unfamiliar with the term might assume that the star tetrahedron is the only merkabah, but just as Kleenex is not the only tissue or Xerox the only copier, there are various forms of the merkabah. We state this because it is important to not create limited thought forms in regard to this. Merkabah does not necessarily mean star tetrahedron, though this certainly is one of the forms one might take.

Currently, the star tetrahedron merkabah is most commonly created through breath and visualization. (This is a very good way to do it.) This is only one method of manifestation, just as there are various ways of manifesting these chariots to produce the many different forms they can take. The most common and frequently utilized form of merkabah manifestation involves the chanting of the divine names of God in the Kaballistic tradition.

For those of you who believe that meditation and mantric chanting are the exclusive rights of the Eastern traditions, we are pleased to inform you that the Western traditions are rich in this heritage as well. In particular, the Kaballistic tradition, dating back thousands of years, taught students to utilize permutations of the holy name of God, derived from the letters of the Tetragrammaton (YHWH), other divine names and vowel sounds, while doing specific visualizations in order to create a merkabah. This has remained among the most esoteric of information until present times and was not taught openly.

Creating Interdimensional Fields

There are numerous ways in which sound can be utilized to open the door and create a gateway to another dimension or level of consciousness. This gateway is the same as a merkabah. Mantric chanting, or repeatedly intoning the name of a god or entity, establishes a resonance field by the intoner (or chanter, if you like). Through this sounding the person creating the sound begins to vibrate to a similar frequency as that of the energy he/she is invoking. It is like the phenomenon of tuning forks, where you can strike one tuning fork and bring it next to another tuning fork of the same frequency and that unstruck tuning fork will begin to sound. Here the chanter, sounding a divine name of an entity and through resonance, begins to attract the entity that he/she was attempting to become. This is the purpose of invoking divine energy.

One of the extraordinary aspects of mantric chanting is

that the names of the different entities and energies are like a sonic formula that matches the resonant frequency of the entity or energy. What occurs is a wonderful example of frequency-shifting. The chanter, in his/her attempt to become one with the divine energy, actually alters his/her vibrational level—shifting frequencies.

Now, let us ask you a question: What does the merkabah, or any dimensional gateway do? They allow a shift in frequencies. Travel to the different planes of consciousness or god levels is simply a matter of frequency-shifting, which can be achieved through sound, light, movement, geometry, crystals and many other modalities (including breathing and visualization). These modalities can be done separately, or they can be combined. It does not matter. What matters is that an individual (or a group) is able to shift frequencies.

The Mayans

It is also possible to travel not only through vibrational levels but great distances using these merkabahs, or gateways. It is thought that the Mayans were able to move from one galactic system to another using the suns of these systems as gateways. How? They would (for want of a better term) "dematerialize" in the heart of the Sun of our system and "rematerialize" in the heart of the sun of another system. This was one way of mass migration. The suns, vibrating at similar frequencies, could be used to create portals from one place to another. It is a bit like transporters in *Star Trek*.

The Mayans also had the ability of intragalactic travel on an individual basis, which did not require such an extreme form of movement. The vehicles (some call them ships) traveling through the sun were for a mass of people. Most of the more highly attuned beings in the different galaxies and dimensions are able to achieve individual (or small group) travel without a vehicle. And mind you, even when a ship is needed, it is frequently not what you would perceive as a tangible object, but actually a unified field created as a group construct or thought form—built by collective group consciousness and not a machine at all.

The gateways to travel to other stars or planes have been known about for many millennia. And as we have said, sound is one of the most preferred means of travel, particularly for small groups. Chanting of divine names has been frequently used. The use of specific vowel sounds, intervals and particular harmonics is also a favored choice of travel, which is now becoming popular again. Both sonic venues utilize visualization along with sound. The harmonically related one might utilize specific geometric forms while the mantric one will most frequently utilize god force visualization. (We discussed the use of mandalas as visualization tools last chapter). Both are equally effective.

What is interesting is that it is possible to transduce (or translate) the mantric/God name chanting to vowel sounds. Neither one is particularly more effective, elevated or evolved. As we suggested earlier, the planes of archetype and geometry coexist and one is not superior to the other.

The key to any sort of transdimensional, interstellar or any similar form of travel is the creation of a gateway. This gateway has been given many names, in many different traditions and on many different worlds. Merkabah is the one that has been the focus of this discussion. Remember, all travel begins with the consciousness and continues with the physical; the basis of all consciousness alteration is shifting frequencies.

◐   ◐   ◐

Chapter 12

Sound, Color and Light

In our last two discussions we delved into the areas of sacred geometry and the construction of inter-dimensional vehicles known as merkabahs. As with all the material thus far presented in "Shifting Frequencies," they represent a small amount of the thought forms inherent in that area. In future discussions we shall present more information on sacred geometry, merkabahs and other related material.

We now would like to touch upon the subject of light and sound. This is an enormous subject to delve into and we can but offer a few thoughts on their being and relationship, as there are many possibilities inherent in the subject of the light-sound interface.

Relationships Between Sound and Light

The relationship between light and sound is most challenging and intriguing because both are measured in frequencies and thus one focus of thought is that light and sound are the same thing. Yet, another school of thought holds that they are quite different entities.

In a nutshell, sound is measured in the tens to the ten

thousands cycles per second. Light travels at millions of miles per hour. When it is measured in the cycles per second, you measure it in the trillions of cycles per second. Therefore, one way to view the relationship is to assume that light is merely speeded up sound, or conversely, sound is merely slowed down light. And on one level, this is true.

The ancient Hermetic principle of "as above, so below" is often quoted in regard to the relationship between sound and light. And mathematically, if you speed up a sound wave's frequency by doubling it forty times, you come up with a frequency that is within the parameters of light. Conversely, if you slow down a light wave's frequency forty times, you have a frequency within the parameters of sound. The frequency of 518.7 cycles per second, which creates a

FREQUENCY RELATIONSHIPS (in cps)

FREQUENCY (x 10²)	COLOR	FREQUENCY DOWN 40 OCTAVES	FREQUENCY (Chromatic)	NOTE
430	Very dark red	391.3	392	G
440	Dark red	400.4		
450	Dark red	409.5		
460	Darkish red	418.6	415	G#
470	Red	427.7		
480	Red-orange	436.8		
490	Orangish red	445.9	440	A
500	Reddish orange	455.0		
510	Light orange	464.1		
520	Yellow	473.2	466	A#
530	Greenish Yellow	482.3		
540	Yellow green	491.4		
550	Yellow green	500.5		
560	Light green	509.6	494	B
570	Green	518.7		
580	Green	527.8		
590	Green	536.9	523	C
600	Bluish green	546.0		
610	Blue green	555.1		
620	Sky blue	564.1		
630	Bluish indigo	573.2	553	C#
640	Indigo	582.3		
650	Indigo	591.4		
660	Indigo	600.5	587	D
670	Indigo violet	609.6		
680	Indigo violet	618.7		
690	Light violet	627.8	622	D#
700	Violet	636.9		
710	Violet	646.0		
720	Dark violet	655.1	659	E
730	Dark violet	664.2		
740	Dark violet	673.3		
750	Very dark violet	682.4	698	F

note somewhat near a C, for example, when speeded up in this manner, falls within the range of what we see as green. Or, when slowed down, this green-colored light that vibrates at 570 trillion cycles per second becomes that note C—at least mathematically. Very dark red vibrates at a frequency of approximately 430 trillion cycles per second, which when reduced by 40 octaves becomes 391.3 cycles per second, creating the note G.

Interestingly, the spectrum of violet goes from light violet at 690 trillion cycles per second (which transduces to 627.8 cycles per second, creating a note somewhere around an E flat) to very dark violet at 750 trillion cycles per second (which transduces to 682.4 cycles per second creating a note close to an F).

According to this system of the relationship between sound and light, then the various aspect of the color violet encompasses E flat, E and F. It provides a wholly different perspective in regard to the puzzle of sound and light. Is it correct or is it merely mathematically mental-plane abstractions, because the question remains: Are sound and light the same? Or are they something different? Jonathan himself had the experience of creating a sound in Palenque, Mexico, during the Harmonic Convergence and having light emerge as a result of this. (This is discussed in greater detail in Jonathan's book Healing Sounds.) The light that was created as a result of Jonathan producing a sound with a harmonic was not a colored light. What occurred instead was that the room Jonathan and his friends were in became slightly illuminated after the sound. The luminosity was enough so that those people in the room could just minimally see each other, when previously all they could perceive was total darkness.

It was Jonathan's thought (through our guidance) that what occurred was not sound turning into light but sound stimulating the pineal, and that gland created a luminosity through the various neurochemicals in the brain—melatonin and so on. Others have also experienced this phenomenon. It even occurs in physics, where it is known as sonoluminescence, which is the experience of sound creating light.

Exercise in Sound Creating Light

If you would like to experience this for yourself, take two quartz crystals and rub them together in a dark room. (Remember to ask their permission first—many crystals do not enjoy this.) You will see an internal glow occur within the crystals, almost as though there were a very dim flashlight in the middle of the crystals. What has occurred is that the crystals transduced the pressure waves (which are basically the same as sound waves) and electrons then are speeded up, eventually creating luminosity. The key word here is "transduced," which means changed from one energy form to another. The sound pressure was not the same as the light that was created—the energy was changed. And as it was changed, it became very different.

When Jonathan first began his journey into sound, he also was directed to begin an understanding of light and the relationship between the two. He found that many different people had expressed very different understandings about the relationship between light and sound. Some perceived specific color relationships with particular keynotes, but invariably these relationships were never the same. The note C was red; it was green; it was purple. It was anything imaginable.

Chakra Colors

We will discuss the relationship between color and the chakras later. But we offer you another question to ponder:

Do you think that the currently regarded rela
ROY G BIV (red, orange, yellow, green, blue, in
and chakras one through seven is a universally agreed upon
principle? We will assure you that it is not. The current (and
expanded) use of the ROY G BIV system of chakra/color
relationship is one that has only come into popularity in the
past few decades. It is a very easy relationship to remember
and because of this, very useful for visualization. And ultimately, if one can flood the body with the different colors of
the rainbow, this can only be of benefit. However, this relationship between the spectrum and the chakras has not been
uniformly agreed upon by anyone. The heart chakra, for
example, would be the color green in the ROY G BIV system. However, some use the color pink for this chakra; others use gold; others, red; others, blues. If you look hard
enough you will find almost any color being used for this
chakra. Here are some suggestions as to why.

First and foremost, what are colors but a perception of the
electromagnetic spectrum. And when one is viewing the
chakras, the question comes into being: Which aspect of the
electromagnetic spectrum is being viewed? Is it from the
etheric level? The emotional level? The mental level? (A different color would be perceived depending upon the level
from which one was viewing.) Different people resonate to
different levels of the electromagnetic spectrum and what
they observe is merely a result of their resonance with this
level.

Second, while there are predominant colors in the chakras,
all colors can be found in each and every chakra. And
depending upon who is being viewed by whom, you will
find a difference in the predominant and secondary colors.
As each person's vibratory frequency of sound might be different, does it not also make sense that perhaps that individual's color scheme might be different?

Synesthesia

Third (and this leads us back to the subject of the relationship between sound and light), we would like to briefly discuss the phenomenon called synesthesia. This is a sensory crossover in which sounds, for example, would be seen as colors (or colors, for another example, smelled). The phenomenon has existed for quite some time, although it is only recently that scientists have given it a name and categorized it (as opposed to dismissing it as being merely a hallucination). Now it is perceived as some sort of strange and unexplainable sensory crossover that occurs. We are pleased that your scientists are now affirming the possibility that certain individuals can see sounds and all sorts of other things. We are sorry to report that while this does occur, there is no more agreement about what colors relate to what sounds (and vice versa) than there was before.

In the past century there were two well-known composers of classical music who both claimed the ability of seeing sounds as colors. And at times they composed for these specifics. A problem, once again, was that neither of these two gentleman were in agreement about what colors specific notes produced. And stories exist that these two beings were in such disharmony with each other over this disagreement that they would get into fisticuffs at sophisticated dinner parties. "C is red!" "No C is green!" "No, it is red!" and so on. It is a humorous example of the human desire to define and own reality.

Thus far no one has ever succeeded in turning a sound wave into a light color without the interference (or should we say, assistance) of a computer or some other instrument. This does not mean there is not a direct relationship between sound and color—there might be. But thus far no one has figured out exactly what it is. Color organs, like those created by the composers we humorously described above, are of course arbitrary assignments of colors to notes. And this is also true of computers that generate colors from sound—there was an arbitrary assignment of these colors by the programmer. It might be that color (light) and sound are two very different energy forms, but we are jumping ahead.

Those of you who have been reading these chapters know that the notes produced by musical instruments and our voices are not pure notes but constructs of sounds created by a fundamental frequency and the harmonics that they produce. Harmonics are mathematical multiples of frequency, so that a fundamental frequency of 100 cycles per second (cps) produces harmonics of 200 cps, 300 cps, 400 cps, 500 cps, 600 cps, 700 cps and so on.

Harmonics and Color

Now, what differentiates the sounds created by your different musical instruments are the most prominent harmonics that they produce. These prominent harmonics (which have been given the name "formants" by your scientists) give musical instruments their timbre, or tone color. While all harmonics are produced whenever a note is sounded, specific harmonics sound more loudly in specific instruments. One instrument might sound a very strong 2nd harmonic and 8th harmonic, while another instrument might sound a very strong 4th harmonic and 6th harmonic. It does not matter what note is being played—the same harmonics will sound loudly depending upon that musical instrument. This again gives the instrument its particular sound.

Now, given the above information, let us assume that there were a very specific relationship between sound and color. Let us just, for example, use the ROY G BIV system in relation to this and apply it to the fundamental so that the note C is red; D is orange; E is yellow; F is green; G is blue; A is indigo; and B is violet. Now, an instrument that, as in our above example, played the note C, but had strong formants of the 2nd and 8th harmonic, which also sounded, would be flashing the color red. There would also be the colors green (2nd harmonic which by using C fundamental produces the note G) and orange (8th harmonic, which by using the C fundamental produces the note D). An instrument that played the note C but had strong formants of the 4th and 6th harmonics would flash the color red. But there would also be a strong yellow (4th harmonics, which by using C fundamental produces the note E) and another strong color which does not fit into this system, since the 8th harmonic produces a note (using C as the fundamental) somewhat less than a B flat. Since B flat falls between the note A (which in our above system would be indigo) and B (which in our system would be violet), let us assume this note creates a mixture of these two colors: indigo/violet.

To reiterate, one instrument plays C and you have red with green and orange. The other instrument, in our example, plays C, and you have red with yellow and indigo/violet. And since sometimes the formants of the harmonics actually sound louder than the fundamental, the associated color (in the above system) would be predominant as well. It is easy to see how, working with the physics of sound, the assignment of colors to notes really creates a rather complicated conundrum of colors in this relationship.

Incidentally, to complicate matters further, we ask you to spend a moment looking around and observing the myriad shades of colors that are available to your eyes. Or better yet, using the memory functions of your brain, remember a time when you walked into a paint store in order to paint a room (or even worse, match a color of some paint). Do you remember how many hundreds of colors you looked at that had blue in them? Or green? Or yellow? Now, we realize there is a difference between pigment and hues, but you get the idea. To say that the note C creates the color red, we ask you: What shade of red? And if you were visualizing a very specific color in your mind and wanted to use a note for this, what note would you use?

It might be that there is a direct relationship of color to sound. But it might be that this relationship is much more complicated than simply taking a note and bringing it up forty octaves to the light-band width. It might be that as sound transduces itself up the electromagnetic spectrum, that as it changes energy, the mathematics become very complicated and different indeed. Jonathan once met a scientist who was working on this and had developed a formula four pages long that transduced sound to color. Whether this formula was correct does not matter, merely that it was another of the extraordinary possibilities inherent in relating color to sound.

Encoding Color on Sound

It is Jonathan's belief, based upon his experience and knowledge, that any color can be carried on any sound. This has basically come about from his teachings, when students would project specific colors that they were visualizing on sounds and those receiving the sounds would also receive the colors that were sent. And it did not matter what the sounds were, the colors that were sent would be received. This indicated to him that colors could be encoded upon sounds, regardless of what the colors and the sounds were.

So, of course, one could encode the note C with the color red. But one could also encode any other color that was desired. We like this system, since it is open-ended—it does not limit one to specific colors or sounds that can be used. The whole spectrum of frequencies is available to be utilized.

If this approach is viable (and we would like to suggest

that it is), then a question remains as to which colors one would use. And we ask you the obvious question: What is your purpose in using the colors? Is it for healing? Transformation? The creation of multidimensional constructs? And if it is for healing, what are you trying to heal (or frequency-shift, as we like to call it)? The physical body? The emotional body? The mental body?

There are excellent books on color and its uses (which do not particularly agree with each other). We suggest that you read them and see what others use for specific situations. And then we ask that you go within, and see what color or colors your inner guidance suggests that you use. There is a certain morphic resonance that has been created by others who have worked in the area of chromatology and chromatherapy. These resonances between the colors and their effects are strong and should be noted.

Many times, for example, the warm colors, such as reds and oranges, have been found to stimulate the physical body, while the cooler colors, such as blue, seem to sedate the physical body. Green is a very healing color, which seems to help regenerate. Violet can be very useful for transmutation of energy. If a part of the body is inflamed, perhaps a blue or turquoise might help it. If the part of the body needs stimulation, perhaps red or orange might assist. But do not get trapped into this system as a be all or end all, because it is merely a possible system that can be used. And once again, as with sound, so with color—it is the intention that you put into the frequency that is as important as the frequency itself.

We realize that we have created a great puzzlement for you in regard to the relationship between sound and color. We have done so for a purpose—for you to begin to understand how the physics of colors and sounds interrelate. And then for you to understand that from a multidimensional viewpoint, this interrelationship (whatever it might be) is indeed only limited to the third dimension and might easily be abandoned in order to work with higher frequencies of color and sound, light and love.

We apologize for any confusion we might have created—it was necessary to show you some of the boxes that you have built. You may now break down these boxes and discard them, realizing that your consciousness will not be inhibited by the previous constraints and constructs. Use whatever systems you like. Explore them. Work with them. Then throw them away when the time is right and when you are ready to move on.

Chapter 13

Sound
and Crystals

Last time we began a discussion on the relationship of sound to color and light. This was a very complicated subject in which we dealt with some of the many aspects of sound and color as they have been used together. In concluding this discussion, we suggested that ultimately any color could be utilized with any sound and vice versa, depending upon the intention and the purpose of those working with these frequencies. This use of sound and light in combination was not the only manner in which these energies could be utilized together. Rather it represented a multidimensional understanding of the subject.

We also suggested that those interested in the relationship of light and color to sound research should study the work of others in this arena. This will enable you to gain a further understanding of the subject from a third-dimensional viewpoint. Many times before one can leap into the alternate dimensions, it is a good idea to become grounded in the dimension you are most familiar with. Before one abandons all constraints and constructs, it is valuable to find out what these constructs are. These constraints and constructs, which might be understood as belief systems or reality bases, can be useful to fall back on in times of indecision and confusion.

Remember the formula, Frequency + Intent = Healing. It is good to know what others have discovered about certain frequencies and how they have used them. If this material resonates with you, then utilize it yourself. If it does not, explore and discover on your own. We are unique vibratory beings and what works for one person might not work for another. This includes sound, light and our next topic, quartz crystals.

We would now like to begin a discussion on quartz crystals and their relationship to sound. What we share with you now is only our perception of the subject. It is not the "Truth" (with a capital "T"), for only you know what is your truth and therefore, the Truth.

Quartz crystals are children of the Earth. They grow in the earth from a silicon dioxide seed, SiO_2. They are gifts from the Earth to help us attune to terrestrial and extraterrestrials. It is all the same. The Earth is a space traveler, just as we are. Quartz crystals assist us in our evolutionary growth upon this and many different planets.

Quartz Crystals

Quartz crystals are considered sacred powerful tools in many of the different traditions and have been recognized as such for a very long time. They have been utilized for their extraordinary abilities by magicians, shamans and lightworkers since recorded history and before as tools for healing, higher consciousness and frequency-shifting. Quartz crystals have been found as artifacts among the most ancient of archeological digs, and their use in Atlantis has been described by many writers.

Quartz crystals have many amazing qualities—perhaps

most extraordinary is their ability to transduce energy. Quartz crystals can take one form of energy and cause it to change form, moving up the energy spiral. Sound, for example, can become electricity, which is called the piezoelectric effect. This phenomenon is real and it is quite discernable on your dimension. Your televisions, radios, stereos and other equipment that play back sound depend upon this phenomenon in order to create sound for you. Do you remember when your record players used a "diamond" needle? This is an example of the piezoelectric effect.

Exercise in Sonoluminescence

Quartz crystals are also sonoluminescent, which means they have the ability to turn sound waves into light. We discussed this briefly last time. If you would like to experience this yourself, take two crystals (ask their permission first, please) and then go into a darkened room. If you rub the crystals together, you will see an internal light coming from the crystals. This is not due to the friction of rubbing quartz crystals together, but is rather an example of the pressure on the crystals (an energy which can be perceived as the wave form of sound), spiraling up the energy octave and being turned into light. It is an amazing phenomenon to witness. This luminescence of crystals might be one of the reasons why "primitive" humans were so interested in crystals. They might have used them as natural flashlights.

Quartz crystals can also hold memory and information—your computers are examples of this. All of your silicon chips in your computers are, of course, quartz. Now, much of the quartz that is used in computers is grown in laboratories and it is slightly different from that which is grown in the earth. It has been said that the laboratory-grown quartz has slightly different qualities and does not seem to hold memory quite as long as naturally grown quartz. Quartz crystals can be programmed by those with knowledge of how to utilize them and this programming can be vast and multidimensional, for quartz crystals are remarkable beings (and beings they are) which can do things in the metaphysical field that would astound many.

Crystals As Holographic Computers

One of your remarkable spiritual scientists who worked with quartz crystals (in this lifetime and in Atlantis) once said that quartz crystals "are holographic computers of the mind." This is very true, for quartz crystals amplify thought forms. As such, the way an individual works with a quartz crystal (and the way that the crystals interface with humans) depends a great deal upon the belief system inherent. It has been said that in regard to quartz crystals, "as you believe, so they behave." This is for the most part, also true.

Many different books have described various different ways for working with and using quartz crystal. Very few of these books say the same thing. This is because crystals amplify thought forms and thus you can encode practically any belief systems into the crystal. For example, when crystals are utilized for healing, they will frequently absorb imbalanced energy that needs to be cleared. With regard to this the varying ways of clearing crystals are amazing. And many of the different teachers are quite regimented about how to clear crystals: "You can only clear crystals with salt water . . . sunlight . . . breath . . . magnets . . ." You get the idea. Many of the different approaches depend upon the tradition, culture and consciousness of the person using the crystal. One thing that all wise users of crystals agree upon is that quartz crystals are sacred and their use should be sacred. This is true.

As we have said, quartz crystals are beings—entities with a consciousness. It might be helpful to think of them as solidified light. They are very willing to merge with human energy fields in order to bring in more light and assist our evolutionary development. They have built within them a basic desire only to be utilized in accordance with that which is sacred from our third-dimensional consciousness—that is the accessing of higher levels of light and love. It is very difficult therefore to misuse a crystal through thought-form amplification. In order to be able to utilize crystals to their maximum ability, it is necessary that the consciousness interfacing with the crystal be oscillating at a very high frequency. In other words, by the time an individual gets to the stage of development where he/she can use a crystal to amplify thought forms, he is operating at such an expanded level of consciousness that the only thoughts he has are in resonance with the crystal.

Quartz crystals have always been in resonance with the sacred. That is why they work so effectively with light, sound geometry and other modalities. They are extraordinary at assisting frequency shifts, for they are natural transducers of energy. And they resonate so effectively with the vibratory nature of humankind.

There are many wonderful books and teachers who work with the energies of quartz crystals. For those of you interested in further exploration of the subject, we would highly recommend searching out these teachers and books. For the moment, we would like to briefly explore some of the ways in which quartz crystals may be utilized for frequency-shifting.

Exercise in Attuning Quartz Crystals

Begin first by holding a crystal comfortably in one of your hands (use one that can be easily held). Then become conscious of your breath, beginning to breathe with the crystal. Breathe in slowly through your nose, hold your breath for a few seconds and then breathe out slowly through your nose. Continue to breathe in this manner for several minutes to fully experience this exercise. The energy of breath is the energy of life. This energy is called many different names by many different traditions: The Hindus called it *prana*, the Orientals called it *chi* or *ki*, the Hebrews called it *ruach*, scientists have called it orgone.

Now, become aware of the change of sensations in the hand that is holding the crystal. By holding a crystal in one of your hands and breathing in this manner, you will create a powerful attunement and resonance with yourself and the quartz crystal. You will find that as you breathe, your body takes on a charge of energy. As you hold your breath, your body builds this charge of energy. Crystals interface wonderfully with the human energy field, so that as you breathe in, the crystal you are holding will also take on this charge of energy and amplify it. As you hold your breath, the crystal will build this charge. As you release your breath, the crystal will also release this charge of energy.

During this exercise, you will become aware of a pulsation in the hand that is holding the crystal. The crystal will begin to pulse with you. Most frequently you will feel the crystal pulse with your breath, expanding as you breathe in, contracting as you breathe out. It is also possible to feel your heartbeat within the crystal, as well as your brain waves in the crystal.

When you pulse with a crystal in this manner, you will be going into very deep states of relaxation. Pulsing with a crystal allows you to be in a state of resonance with a crystal and is helpful in accessing higher dimensions. A feedback loop occurs. As you slow your breath and begin to bring your consciousness to the crystal, it will also be working with you, assisting you in reaching higher states of consciousness. It is a very powerful experience.

Always remember that crystals are merely tools to be utilized for frequency-shifting. They are a means to an end, but not an end to themselves. The techniques that can be learned through working with crystals are just that—techniques. These techniques can ultimately be achieved by humans working by themselves without any assistance. But quartz crystals are wonderful teachers of the process of learning to shift our frequencies.

Crystals can hold the "programs," or the intentions of their user. By their own nature, crystals will assist in creating balance and heightening consciousness in the individuals who utilize them. When sacred intention is projected into a crystal using thought, breath or sound, the focused energy of the crystal is amplified. This is because crystals can act as holographic computers of the mind. The intention or program you put into a crystal can virtually be anything you can think of, as long as it is aligned with divine light and love.

Crystals can be utilized in many different ways for the process of achieving balance and alignment. Merely by holding a crystal over a chakra with the intention of that crystal balancing the chakra, this effect will be achieved. This is one reason why people frequently wear crystals. Wearing crystals helps to balance the auric field in particular and the area around the heart chakra or thymus, where these crystals are often worn.

A very powerful method of crystal healing involves using crystals as a tool to remove imbalanced or stuck energy in the etheric field. Since this is a very advanced technique, we will not elaborate upon the process at this time. We state its existence for those of you who wish to contemplate avenues of exploration with a crystal.

Creating Crystal Grids

When a number of crystals are arranged together, they are

Figure A.
Star of David
Gridwork

Figure B.
Double
Star of David
Gridwork

Figure C.
Pentagon/
Pentagram
Gridwork

Figure D.
Octagon
Gridwork

Figure E.
Decagon
Gridwork

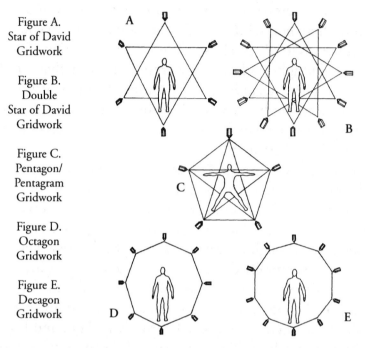

excellent at helping create various energy fields. This is done through using the crystals in specific numbers and arranging them in specific geometric forms, which is called a crystal grid. One of the easiest to work with is the Star of David configuration, in which six crystals of similar size are used. The crystals are arranged in a pattern so that six of them are placed at the points of a hexagon with terminations (points) pointed inward. It is helpful if the two triangles that create this Star of David are connected with your consciousness.

Since crystals are hexagonal by nature, in essence what you have created by aligning the crystals in this configuration is a very large etheric crystal. In the center of this crystal grid the energy comes together in a short time to form a pillar of light. It is an excellent place for frequency-shifting. Listening to sacred music or creating sacred sound in such a crystal gridwork will enhance the energy of the grid and is highly recommended.

We suggest that those of you who are interested create one of these Star of David configurations and then sit or lie in the middle of the grid. Try it for a short time and experience what happens. It is quite excellent for enhancing states of deep meditation, visualization and interdimensional journeying. The pillar-of-light effect in the center of the gridwork is a very powerful field that will assist in raising the vibrations of the individual within it. This configuration is an excellent addition to places of healing and frequency-shifting. And yes, this gridwork might also create a merk-abah, if that is the intention of the field being generated.

As always, with any frequency-shifting technique or tool, it is highly suggested that one approach this use of crystals with caution and do not overdo it. Initially we recommend spending only fifteen minutes in this crystal-grid formation and seeing its effect upon you. Gradually, if appropriate, you might build up the time that you spend. There are some individuals who have created crystal grids under their beds and they love it. But these individuals have built up their vibrational rate to the level where this energy can be handled.

The Star of David configuration is only one of many geometric forms that can be created by using quartz crystals. Each configuration will be different, since the effects of each geometry is different. Honor the energy of the crystals that you are working with and of yourself. If it feels appropriate, experiment with different geometric crystal grids and experience their effect. It will be most rewarding.

When crystals are used for healing they can absorb imbalanced energy, which makes them excellent tools for aligning energy. It is important, however, to clear the crystal. What occurs is that crystals vibrate at extremely high frequencies of light. When they absorb imbalanced energy, this energy becomes stuck in the crystal and the normal vibratory rate of

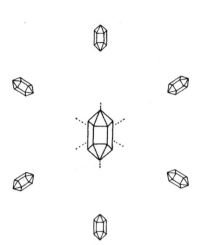

Star of David gridwork system

the crystal changes. As such, it is necessary to clear the crystal to release this energy. Use whatever method of crystal clearing that you feel resonant with. Jonathan likes to use sound, though all methods work well. The use of sound with crystals is an extremely effective and powerful way of working with quartz. It is a subject that we will discuss next time, including the phenomenon of crystal singing.

🌀   🌀   🌀

Chapter 14

Crystal Singing

ast time we began a discussion on quartz crystals as tools for frequency-shifting. We briefly discussed programming and clearing, offering suggestions on how crystals can be pulsed and how crystal gridworks can be created. We continue with the relationship of sound to crystals.

Crystals can be cleared, then charged and programmed with sound and continue to hold those encoded frequencies. They can also be cut to hold specific frequencies and be shaped to different geometries. And one can sing with them—we call this crystal singing.

Jonathan has been working with quartz crystals for as many years as he has worked with sound. He watched as they came into what could be called New Age consciousness, then disappeared for a while. They are now coming back into popularity. It has been an interesting journey that might fill a book. The relationship between quartz crystals and sound is a fascinating avenue to explore.

Crystal Singing

It is said that every crystal is alive with its own sound.

Some highly sensitive people can actually tune in to these natural frequencies and hear them sing. Those with the desire and ability can learn to sing into the crystals to create harmonics that match their frequencies. We call this crystal singing, and it can lead one into greater attunement with crystals. It can also amplify the power of both participants, and by focusing it one can use crystals as tools for transformation and healing.

The use of sound (sonics) has long been overlooked in crystal work, yet sonics played a significant role in crystal use in ancient times. In these healing temples, trained people sang into crystals, with astounding results. In Atlantis healer-priests would arrange themselves in specific geometric patterns around an individual. By singing into the crystals, organs and limbs could be regenerated. In those ancient times crystals were cleared, programmed and energized with healing energy by sound, the energy then transmitted through the voice and amplified, focused and converted into higher forms through the crystal. We are now slowly returning to this knowledge.

Each crystal has its own resonant frequency based on the shape, structure, density and size of the crystal. This frequency differs from its molecular frequency, which is the same for all crystals and is created subatomically. The resonant frequency we speak of is that which can be matched sonically by the human voice, in essence the same as that emitted by the crystal.

Jonathan discovered this phenomenon one day many years ago when he was sounding into a crystal. To his amazement, as he projected different vocal harmonics into it, he found that it amplified specific harmonics. When he picked up another crystal, he found that different harmonics were amplified. Puzzled by this discovery, he checked with several other people to see if they also experienced this phenomenon. They did.

Jonathan then called a well-known scientist who researched and worked with crystals. This scientist validated the effect and congratulated Jonathan on rediscovering an ancient technique. Through experimenting with  his own sound, Jonathan learned how to create a resonance with a crystal. Both Jonathan and the crystal were in effect singing together.

Vocal Harmonics

The key to developing an ability to match the resonant frequency of a crystal lies in vocal harmonics. (Several earlier chapters have discussed this subject, also known as overtone chanting and harmonics singing.) This refers to the ability of the human voice to refract sound so that not only is the fundamental frequency of the voice heard, but also the many harmonics that lie within the sound spectrum of any one note.

The creation of vocal harmonics, initially utilized by Tibetan Buddhists and Mongolian shamans, is now becoming both an art form and a frequency-shifting modality here in the West. Vocal harmonics are powerful tools: They can resonate the physical body and the etheric fields; entrain brain waves, stimulating and charging the brain; improve the quality of the voice and enhance the ability to hear. They are excellent tools for meditation and heightened consciousness and can be used to create interdimensional vehicles. And they are also beautiful to listen to.

Creating vocal harmonics is discussed in detail in *Healing Sounds*. One key is sounding different sacred vowels. Although a trained harmonic singer can create a dozen or more overtones from any note and focus the energy of each of these tones, you don't need such training to use harmonics effectively with crystals.

Since quartz crystals can themselves amplify the specific harmonics they resonate to, you need only a rudimentary ability for harmonics to practice crystal singing. Once you know how to sound a harmonic, you need to scan vocally the crystal. By toning up and down the scale while you project harmonics, you will find at least one frequency (there are usually several due to the mathematical nature of the harmonic series) in which one harmonic becomes louder. If you are holding the crystal in your hand, you will feel it begin to vibrate and pulse. This tells you that the natural resonant frequency of the crystal has been matched by your voice, and the crystal begins to sing.

Clearing and Programming

When you concentrate on that frequency and project different harmonics, several extraordinary things will occur. By matching the resonant frequency of a crystal, you cause the crystal to vibrate to its highest natural state of being. When this occurs, negative programming or vibrations within the crystal are eliminated. The crystal is cleared when it returns to its own highest natural state. It also becomes energized and activated, since you are helping the crystal to amplify its own natural vibratory rate.

Sound is energy, and when an individual puts this energy into the crystal, it amplifies, converts and transmutes this energy to a higher form. When used for healing, the person holding and singing into a crystal will project the harmonics into a facet near its base. The crystal takes this sound energy, amplifies it and transmits it through the point. It also converts this energy into much higher octaves and transmits that as healing light through the point of the crystal as well.

When another person is involved, the effects can be extremely powerful. Sound, light and other energies can be focused upon someone who needs healing. Crystal singing is a variation of the overtoning technique, which Jonathan describes in Healing Sounds. Using a crystal, however, adds other elements of the electromagnetic spectrum to sound.

You can program a crystal with this method: While the crystal is vibrating in its highest natural state, simply project the intended program into your sound. This new program will be sonically encoded into it. [See first illustration.] Clearing these programs has already been discussed.

When a person is crystal singing, resonance is created between the singer and the crystal. This resonance attunes the singer with the crystal, regardless of the techniques. Often one can get out of sync with a crystal due to stress or other problems. But crystals can also get out of sync when they are transported long distances, because their attunement to one area might be out of sync in another, like some kind of crystal jet lag. However, crystal singing can reattune the crystal to the new geographical location. As always, keep in mind that crystal singing is sacred. Because it works with the highest essence of sound and light, it cannot be used for any other purpose.

Sonic Encoding

Quartz crystals can be sonically encoded to resonate to specific frequencies. One way is to cut it to a particular frequency. An easier method is simply exposing it to the frequency it wishes to encode. Any frequency can potentially be encoded into a quartz crystal, particularly ones that can

be used for healing and vibrational shifting. Tuning-fork frequencies can be encoded into a crystal simply by holding the vibrating tuning fork near it. Frequencies that are encoded on tapes and by other electronic means can also be encoded into crystals via headphones or stereo speakers by placing the crystal between the headphones or flat on a speaker. While it is potentially possible to encode almost any frequency into a crystal at least temporarily, we suggest that you use great discretion and discernment in choosing which sounds you work with.

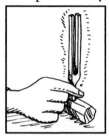

Since crystals are sacred by their very nature, different sacred sounds and mantras can be sonically encoded into quartz crystals. This is done through sounding directly into it. You can carry or wear a crystal that has been encoded to alleviate an imbalance or that resonates to a specific sacred mantra. Needless to say, the effects would be extremely beneficial.

Sacred Sounds

Sacred sounds are also effective in clearing crystals of imbalanced energies. Sounding an om, for example (replete with harmonics), is a wonderful method of helping a crystal resonate with sacred energies. The use of Tibetan bowls and bells is another way to clear crystals. Years ago Jonathan worked with a doctor friend who was very skilled in kinesiology (using muscle testing to determine if something is beneficial for the person being tested). They worked with tuning forks, Tibetan bells (called ting-shas) and Tibetan bowls. Tuning forks had subjective effects; some frequencies were beneficial, others were not. However, Tibetan bells and bowls seemed to create beneficial effects, regardless of the frequencies. Jonathan surmised that this was because the bells and bowls had been encoded with sacred intention when they were cast.

In recent times bowls have also been made of silicon dioxide — wonderful instruments that have very profound effects. These crystal bowls, when vibrating, produce very pure tones that are excellent for clearing unbalanced energies. They are, of course, wonderful for simply making sounds. It is interesting that the creators of these bowls make them in different frequencies for the different chakras. But different manufacturers and users cannot seem to agree upon which frequencies should be used with which chakras. Should C be used for the first chakra, or A? We would like to suggest that the tones of these bowls are so pure that with the proper attention and intention, any bowl can balance and align any chakra. As with any instrument, much of the effect of the sound is based on the focus given by the individuals who create and receive the sound. Crystal bowls are marvelous tools that affect the body, the brain and the etheric fields of people nearby, clearing and charging their energy.

Grid Alignment

Jonathan recently decided to teach sound and crystals to his students at his Healing Sounds Intensive. He presented the crystal singing technique, which he had not taught for over a decade. An unexpected and extraordinary effect occurred, which Jonathan had been unaware of. An interdimensional grid, sometimes called the axiatonal grid, was affected in the individual lying in the center of the circle. This geometric energy grid, which surrounds each person, was aligned and activated. This happened quite naturally without any previous training and was a result of sacred sound interfacing with the crystals. This is very effective for both personal and planetary activation—very effective.

Jonathan was perhaps most amazed that this gridwork alignment had not occurred a decade before when he had taught crystal singing. It was an astounding and exciting new experience. The encodement of these grids is the result of new energy alignments that have only recently manifested on this planet. A morphic resonance has been created through this grid activation, allowing the encodement of the grids through certain beings who can channel this energy, whether or not they are fully conscious of this energy. It is an example of the higher planes working through the physical and a continued indication of the experiences that are occurring as the frequencies shift.

We suggest that those interested in exploring the relationship between sound and crystals begin by working with your own sound, gaining awareness of your voice as a tool for resonance and frequency-shifting. Then begin to work with quartz crystals, pulsing and resonating with them [see last chapter] but still working with your own sound. After you feel comfortable with both your own sounds and the vibrations of crystals, you can combine them with crystal singing to experience their mutually enhancing effects. You will discover many extraordinary things about both quartz crystals and yourself as you practice.

ⓦ　　ⓦ　　ⓦ

Chapter 15

Breath

In this discussion we would like to talk about what might be the simplest, easiest and most frequently ignored aspect of frequency-shifting that is available to you: breath. We have briefly discussed the importance of breath in previous conversations, but we would like to go into more detail at this time.

The Breath of Life

The energy of breath is the energy of life; the energy of life is the energy of breath. Without breath there truly is no life—at least for beings on this planet. Your life begins with an inbreath—the first noble inspiration—and your life ends with an outbreath — the last noble expiration. Breath is life; life is breath. It is that simple.

The energy inherent in breath has been known in spiritual and healing traditions for countless millennia. Hindus call this *prana;* Orientals call it *chi* or *ki;* Hebrews call it *rauch,* which is also their word for spirit. A modern spiritual scientist called it *orgone.* This energy goes under a hundred different names in a hundred different languages and traditions, but it is the same energy, the energy of life.

When you inhale your body and energy field take on this charge of energy. As you hold your breath, your body builds this charge. When you exhale, your body releases this charge of energy, only to start all over again. This energy supplies nutrients to the body and the brain and supports the release of toxins.

Some of your scientists, particularly the spiritual scientists, have studied the effects of the breath. We recommend reading various books on the subject, for the information and material is too vast to be covered here.

Breath Techniques

Different types of breathing stimulate different subtle changes. Some variables are breathing through the nostrils versus breathing through the mouth; assuming different postures with different breathing techniques; the timing of the breath; different methods of inhalation; and various visualizations that can be imprinted on the breath. All these variables affect different aspects of the physical self (nerves, brain and so on) and the subtle bodies.

Many important meditation techniques from different traditions focus on the breath alone. Through observing one's breathing, great insights into the self are achieved. In essence, one sits and breathes while clearing the mind of everything but the conscious act of breathing. It sounds easy, but it is an enormous task. This breathing is usually done slowly, in and out through the nose.

Different methods of breathing seems to induce different altered states. While slow, rhythmic breathing through the nose is used for one type of meditation, fast, shallow breathing is used for another. Their purposes are different, as are the physiological effects. The body and brain produce different chemicals through the different practices.

Should one breathe through the nose or the mouth?

These too produce different effects. Breathing through the nose stimulates the parasympathetic nervous system and elicits what is known as the relaxation response. It reduces heart rate, respiration and brain waves and therefore reduces stress.

Breathing through the mouth is energizing, stimulating the nervous system. However, when done habitually, it seems to elicit the fight-or-flight response. We do not suggest that mouth breathing—such as when one is toning or chanting—is not useful. It has specific purposes that can be quite powerful. However, when habitually used to the virtual exclusion of nostril breathing, its overall effect is stressful.

Within the nose-breathing arena itself are many different systems, including a technique in which an individual breathes in and out through alternate nostrils. Inhaling through the left nostril stimulates the right hemisphere; inhaling through the right nostril stimulates the left hemisphere. When alternating the nostrils on the inbreath and outbreath, an individual balances the two hemispheres.

The results of different breathing techniques are unique, each technique having its own purpose. You can imagine that rapid, shallow breathing would be stimulating and dizziness might result. But it can be a cleansing breath. Fast, shal-

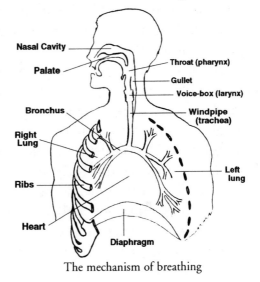

The mechanism of breathing

low breathing is not a technique that can be practiced for a long time, but it has power when used specifically for an intended purpose. Slow, deep breathing produces a relaxed clarity.

Deep Breathing

We would like to suggest that for most beings on planet Earth it is important at this time to learn to develop what is frequently called deep breathing. This is a natural breath; if you observe infants, you will see that when they are in a relaxed state, their bellies will rise on the inbreath. For reasons that are not obvious to us, as humans grow and mature, particularly in your Western culture, they begin to breathe shallowly, taking in less oxygen and prana (energy nutrition) into the body and brain. Their life energy is reduced and they become more susceptible to stress.

Shallow breathing is quite common and makes little sense—as little as many other self-destructive behaviors prevalent on your planet at this time. Why, we ask, would you forget how to breathe when the life energy of the cosmos is inherent in the breath? We are pleased that so many are beginning to remember the importance of breath and are teaching this to others.

This deep-breathing technique involves simply taking a slow, deep breath through the nose and allowing the air to expand into all parts of your lungs. Take a deep breath through the nose while placing a hand on the belly and see what happens. Pay particular attention to where the air goes. For most people, the difficulty arises in bringing the air all the way to the diaphragm. Bring the air down as far as possible into your lungs and notice whether your belly moves outward. Notice whether your shoulders go up when you inhale deeply. If they do, relax them.

Many children were taught in grade school a "belly in,

shoulders out" technique for breathing. While this gets a bit more air into the upper chest, most of the breath is lost to the lower belly. We cannot understand why this technique would be taught, other than it makes one look more "powerful" (in terms of your Western martial standard). It certainly is not a relaxed breath, nor is it particularly comfortable. But it does look good if you wish to parade around on the beach trying to impress someone.

Exercise in Deep Breathing

Try taking a deep breath through the nose so that the air flows into all parts of your lungs, especially the lower part. Breathe in to the count of four (four seconds), then hold to the count of four. Then release the breath slowly through the nose, again to the count of four. This will take about four seconds from the time you begin an exhale till all the air is out of your lungs. After the exhale remain in a state of stillness for about four seconds. Then after another count of four, begin the cycle again. Do this for several breath cycles and see what happens. If you have never breathed in this manner before, you might find it is transformative.

A slow, deep breath brings precious oxygen and life energy to the body and brain. It slows down the heartbeat and brain waves, helping induce deep relaxation and calm. It reduces stress and enhances health. Why would anyone breathe in a different manner?

Deep breathing is an important aspect of shifting one's frequency. The slower and more relaxed are the oscillations of the human brain and the heartbeat, the greater the frequencies of light and love that are encoded into the physical and etheric bodies. In other words, it is easier for humans to handle higher frequencies when they are calm and relaxed. This is one of the results of meditation and other forms of shifting one's consciousness.

Color Breathing

Once you have begun to master deep breathing, additional energies and focuses of consciousness can be encoded onto the breath. Visualization is one of these. You can begin by visualizing color on the breath (sometimes called color breathing). Breathe in while visualizing a particular color, thereby encoding it into the breath where it will enter the physical and subtle bodies. As the breath is held, continue to visualize the color penetrating to the molecular level and radiating outward to the etheric level.

White light, composed of all colors, is an excellent one to begin with. Visualize radiant white light penetrating the physical and etheric levels. White light brings divine nutrition to the cells and DNA. Just imagine the frequency-shifting that occurs!

More complex visualizations can be used with the breath. Imprinting different geometric forms on the inbreath is another way to shift frequencies. The geometric form can be visualized as penetrating a particular portion of the body, or else the body and etheric fields can be within the large geometric form. Or both might be used simultaneously. Some people work effectively with the star tetrahedron in this manner. Visualizing particular shapes—usually platonic solids (such as the triangle or diamond)—activate specific portions of the brain.

Different colors and geometric forms have different effects, depending on the individual and his/her resonance. It is suggested that you experiment with different combinations of colors and geometric forms and observe the results. The intention that you imprint on the different colors and geometries will also affect your results.

Intention is extremely important in any aspect of frequency-shifting. Our old formula of *frequency + intent = healing* still applies. Here we are dealing with the principle that the breath is the carrier wave of consciousness. Intentionality rides on the breath. It has been suggested that the ideal place to program intentionality is at the still point between the inbreath and the outbreath. While this is not the only place to program intention, it is certainly an excellent place. Some systems that work with visualization and sound, such as mantras, will actually have you visualize the sound while taking an inbreath—for example, breathing in the "Om Mani Padme Hum" sound before actually chanting it. This undoubtedly increases the charge being encoded on both the breath and the sound, making the mantra even more effective.

Breath and Sound

A next step in working with breath involves the factor of sound. From our perspective, breath is the basis of sound. There can, of course, be no self-created vocal sound without breath. It is impossible for a human to create vocal sound without using the breath. Many traditions use the breath as an actual sound. For example, in the Hindu tradition, the "so-ham" mantra has a person focus his/her consciousness on the sound "so" as one breathes in and "ham" as one breathes out. It is interesting to note that sometimes, this mantra is reversed (called the "ham-so" mantra) and you focus "ham" on the inbreath and "so" on the outbreath. The effects of these two mantras, which rely exclusively upon intentionality and the sound of the breath, resonant quite differently. Resonance through the sound of the breath alone can massage glands within the brain, thus stimulating the secretions of nectar of metamorphosis or consciousness-shifting.

You can begin this breathing by gently increasing the sound of the breath. Through slightly changing the pressure of your breath, the shape of the mouth cavity and other variables, the audible sound changes. It might become louder or softer, higher pitched or lower pitched, depending on your desire or intent. Imagine yourself as a creator being, breathing the universe into existence. This is a wonderful tool for learning to use a gentle, soft sound in a powerful and expansive way.

Another exercise is to focus on a particular part of the body while breathing in. When you experiment with this, become aware of the increased flow of energy to the part of the body you are breathing to. It is possible to channel the sound of the breath through specific energy pathways, such as the meridians, or nadis. Breath can travel on these pathways as easily as it can travel to specific organs and areas of the body.

You might even learn to breathe in through the top of your head and out through the bottoms of your feet—or vice versa. This is a powerful way to circulate the energies of the cosmos and the Earth. One can learn to breathe through the chakras as well. Adding sound to the breath—for instance, an "ah" sound, riding upon the breath while breathing through the heart chakra—is a way to draw in, then radiate, the energy of love. Experiment with this and other sounds when you have the opportunity. It is very powerful and quite enjoyable.

The possibilities for using the breath to move energy, increase vitality and shift frequencies is practically endless. Breath is life. It is also divine sound, divine light and divine love. It has been with you since the beginnings of this planet. For many, it has been taken for granted. We suggest that you honor your breath and yourselves as an aspect of divine consciousness. Breathe the light. Be the light. It can only assist you.

ⓦ   ⓦ   ⓦ

Chapter 16

The Waveform Experience

L ast time we discussed the wonder of breath and its use for shifting frequency. This time we will focus on the inward and outward movement of the breath—its waveform.

Waveform As Frequency

If you pluck a string, it vibrates up and down. This upward and downward movement of the string creates a wave. Frequency is one measurement of this movement of a vibrating object. Frequency is usually measured in how many waves per second an object vibrates. However, this movement, or periodicity, might take far longer than seconds to complete a cycle. The breath too displays waveform characteristics, but its rhythms create a sound whose frequency is measured in cycles per minute. If you clap your hands once a second, you create a frequency of one cycle a second.

Humans hear frequencies from about 16 to around 16,000 cycles per second as sound. However, just because something vibrates slower or faster than this (and therefore falls outside the human auditory range) does not mean it is not creating a sound, only that the human ear cannot hear it.

Objects that vibrate below our normal range of hearing are usually felt rather than heard.

Some waveforms are incredibly fast, such as those of the electron orbiting the nucleus of an atom; and some are incredibly slow, such as a planet orbiting a sun. Both objects—the electron and the planet—display waveforms despite the fact that the frequencies they create are beyond the normal level of human perception.

The idea of the waveform can be used to describe the way things work in this universe. Oceans display waveform characteristics, though not as easy to observe and as precise as that of a vibrating string. The ancient Chinese incorporated this concept into a circle, creating the yin/yang Taoist symbol.

We would also like to use it as a metaphor for life. (Don't forget that any metaphor is only a partial truth. The phenomena surrounding waveforms describe only a part of this universe, so other universes must exist that don't have them at all.)

One of Jonathan's favorite examples comes from observing traffic (particularly relevant when you are attempting to cross a street). There might be no cars for five minutes, then as if from nowhere, there is bumper-to-bumper traffic followed again by no traffic.

Caught in a crowd? Wait a little while and see what happens. The odds are that the waveform cycle will be observable and there will be moments of few or no people. "When it rains, it pours," is a description of this phenomenon, as is "it's either feast or famine."

This is observable in many other areas of life. A Zen koan describes it: "First there is a mountain. Then there is no mountain. Then there is."

The Flow of the Wave

An understanding of the waveform means to understand

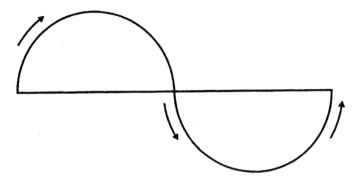

A wave form

that all things change, that nothing is static. Such a realization can help individuals caught up in uncomfortable situations. With this understanding, the darkness of a situation will not seem quite so dark, because you know that the light will once again appear. Observing waveform phenomena can lessen one's reaction to and judgment of outer events.

The waveform represents the ebb and flow of the universe, observable in tides and traffic or just about everything else. How many of you get in a down spot in your lives and think, Well, this is just temporary and things will undoubtedly go up in a little while. Instead, you think, Things are really down—and that is where your consciousness stays. You would probably feel much better if you realized that, like the vibration of a string, what goes up must go down.

When Buddha spoke of the impermanence of things, he was on one level observing the waveform. This can also be observed in the wheel of life of the Buddhist tradition. Things cannot be permanent, because they are like waves (in fact, they are waves). Ultimately winter moves to spring moves to summer moves to fall moves to winter again.

By pointing out the phenomenon of the waveform, we hope that life will become easier for some of you. By observing and understanding it, you will begin to see it operate in your life.

Rarely in your waveform cycles does a wave become stuck. The waveform is a helpful metaphor because it does not easily lend itself to black/white, either/or labels. On your planet the genderfication (division into two polarities) of most objects and attributes seems to be an ongoing occupation for many, seeing things as either masculine or feminine—even energy and sound spin.

The Genderfication of Sound

A major duality is male and female, so let us examine what we call the "genderfication" of sound. Here we are being playful, although we hope it can be nevertheless useful. This line of thought resulted from a question at one of Jonathan's recent workshops: "Is sound masculine or feminine?" Jonathan laughed when he heard the question—not because it made no sense, but because it did make sense. When he asked, "Why do you ask?" the person responded that a teacher had referred to certain energetic spins as masculine and other spins as feminine and wondered if this description could be applied to sound. Jonathan briefly explored application of polarity to sound. We would like to share this with you.

Sound in the physicalized world began with the creation of single notes. Were these fundamental notes feminine and their harmonics masculine, or vice versa? When notes are put together to create a scale, are accidentals masculine and the notes of the scale feminine, or vice versa? What about intervals (the distance between two notes)? Is a fourth (for example, a C and the F above) masculine and a fifth (for example, a C and the G above) feminine, or vice versa? Are major chords masculine and minor chords feminine, or vice versa?

This inquiry continued into musical instruments. Could they be divided into masculine and feminine—the violin, for example, being feminine and the oboe perhaps masculine? Then the question of whether vowels were masculine and consonants feminine (or vice versa) began. Are words masculine and melodies feminine, or are melodies masculine and harmonies feminine? It became quite comical as the different possible dualities were examined. Jonathan ended with the concepts of sound and silence. Is silence feminine and sound masculine, or vice versa? Someone could spend an enormous amount of time and energy playing with it, probably even write a book on the subject.

From a plane of nonduality, you can see how amusing such a discussion would be. In duality, however, there really is some merit to these questions in the world of sound, since it might be possible to create guidelines for what is masculine and what is feminine essence, then create even further division for a better understanding.

We suggest that analogs include gender and genderfication. Even within you humans, gentlemen have much female and females have much male. It is simply the way things are. You have a mixture of masculine and feminine chromosomes. Yes, there is usually a predominance of one or the other (when it has an equal balance, a hermaphrodite results, considered sacred in ancient times), but it is rarely black or white, either/or.

We further suggest that attributes such as expansive for masculine and contractile for feminine (or vice versa) are limiting concepts. They might be useful for defining and understanding energy, but they are too confusing, constrictive and judgmental when applied literally to your lives. They can limit your beliefs and understanding of the different realities you are constructing.

Constricting your thought forms is not the purpose of shifting frequency. This leaves you in the dualistic position of "this is this, that is that," from which you cannot step further, having fully defined your reality. Understanding the waveform can help you see that "this seems to be this on the way to becoming that," so that you don't get locked into static beliefs. Fluidity is an integral element of shifting frequencies, and an understanding of waveform cycles can lead to fluidity.

ⓦ   ⓦ   ⓦ

Chapter 17

Harmony

W e have dealt with many different aspects of vibration, including light, crystals, sacred geometry, breath and, of course, sound. This time our focus is on harmonics.

We would like to begin our discussion of harmony by suggesting that above the level of duality there truly are no harmonious and disharmonious sounds. All sounds, from a divine perspective, are harmonious. Yet if harmony means being in balance with nature, then certainly much is out of balance.

Harmonics

As sonic encodements, harmonics provides a natural harmony with which one can resonate. In the harmonic series, geometric multiples of a given fundamental frequency (which are usually not heard consciously, but contribute to the tone color), the further one progresses up the series, the more dissonant-sounding they seem.

In the harmonic (or overtone) series the first harmonic creates an octave, vibrating twice as fast as the fundamental. In the key of C the fundamental is a C and the first har-

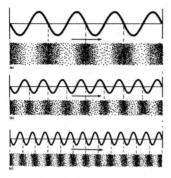

Sound waves in harmonic ratios.

monic is the C an octave above. The second harmonic creates a note that vibrates three times as fast as the fundamental. When this note is played with the first harmonic, it creates the musical ratio of 2 to 3, an interval we call a fifth. In the key of C this is a C and the G above. Many consider this ratio the most harmonious ("consonant") interval.

The third harmonic is the C an octave above the last, vibrating four times as fast as the fundamental C. The fourth harmonic vibrates five times faster than the fundamental frequency. In the key of C this is the E above the previous C. The last two notes generated create an interval of a major third.

The fifth harmonic vibrates six times faster than the fundamental and is the G an octave above the previous G. These all sound harmonious when played together. However, in continuing up the series, the intervals sound more and more disharmonious (dissonant).

The Blue Note

The sixth harmonic generates a note vibrating seven times faster than the fundamental. In the key of C it is a flatted seventh (Bb). This note is frequently heard in jazz and blues, and has been called a "blue" note. Many find it a moving sound. However, when the blue note began to be used in unexpected chord progressions by the turn of last century, it caused great consternation. Not only was this note (and the music that embodied it—jazz) dismissed as dissonant, it was also judged "bad," some even describing it as demonic and apt to cause insanity. The blue note was accused of creating

many unwanted conse-
quences. Riots were feared if
people were to hear this
sound in a room together.
(No doubt the downfall of
Western civilization was the
result.)

The blue note might have
caused such a reaction because it ushered in a new realm of
sonic consciousness. Those attuned to earlier music were
unable to accept this note, especially those who had based
their sonic reality upon progressions traditionally used in
classical music. To these people, the blue note was an
unwanted radical that shook up not only music structure,
but the structure of consciousness. Nowadays, of course,
Western musicians frequently bring in this and other "dissonant" frequencies without risking riot. We ask you, did the
sound itself change, or did people's perception of it change?

It has been suggested that as humankind's listening
changes and evolves, the human nervous system (and consciousness) will be able to incorporate the higher harmonics
of the overtone series. Many readers can remember the
music they enjoyed in their youth (probably to the dismay of
their parents) and realize it is now incorporated into the culture. Many of you are parents now and are having difficulty in appreciating (dare we say tolerating?) the music your
children listen to. Remember that your children are simply
stretching the sonic envelope to expand your reality of what
is acceptable sound. It is a great service they are doing for
you, as you did for your parents and your parents did for
their parents.

The Upper Overtone Series

Many years ago Jonathan attended a presentation on

exploring the upper overtone series given by a wonderful teacher and explorer of sound. This teacher had programmed a synthesizer so that it played notes in the overtone series. These notes, however, were not ones normally perceived by our ears (which usually do not hear harmonics beyond the first dozen or so), notes as high as the sixty-fourth and sixty-fifth overtone.

When the two overtones are played together, it sounds much like the buzzing of insects. It is actually a very pleasant sound if one can become fluid and resonate with its energy. We suggest that those interested in exploring natural interdimensional fields listen to crickets, insects, frogs and other creatures that make sounds together in nature. These creatures might have knowledge worth investigating about creating fields via sound.

A question arises as to whether all sounds are harmonious with the human energy field. The truth is, some sounds are not; some might even be destructive unless the consciousness of the individual is sufficiently evolved to transform them into something benevolent. While sounds such as the interval of the fifth (the C to G) balance the nervous system, some sounds (such as a chainsaw) are not very soothing to the mind, body or spirit—at least from your present level of consciousness.

Dissonance

Be aware, however, that dissonant sounds have a purpose. In the chaos it creates, dissonance can shake up static energy and allow transformation to occur if one can stay fluid when encountering their energy.

Fluidity

If a person is rigid when encountering a field that seems disharmonious, he is like a board in a strong wind: eventually the board will snap. However, if a person is like a blade of grass that bends in the wind, these fields will cause no damage. This, of course, is one of the major purposes of both fluidity and frequency-shifting. Sound can teach us how to be fluid. If we can learn to listen to and feel dissonant sound without being adversely affected by it, that is truly an advancement in consciousness. (It is also, we admit, quite difficult.)

For instance, some find the sounds of a refrigerator disturbing. If you are one of these, the next time you hear a refrigerator, use your imagination and transform the sound—perhaps to the deep chanting of Tibetan monks or a similarly peaceful image. The roar of a jet plane can be transformed into the sound of huge ocean waves. Sonic transformation is often effective in changing the way certain sounds affect us. But this can be difficult, particularly if the sound is a jackhammer outside your window!

One reason why jackhammers, chain saws and similar machine-created sounds are so destructive to most human senses is simply because they are too loud. These machines have an amplitude outside normal human tolerance. They certainly exceed the level of sound found in nature, like crickets, frogs, birds and most mammals. However, sounds such as the songs of humpback whales can actually surpass in decibel level the loudness of jackhammers and chain saws. We suggest that the intention of these machine sounds and those who use them do not incorporate the energies of light and love, so they are not beneficial to living fields. Here is a story that might shed light on how sonic transformation can occur unexpectedly.

An Experience in Fluidity

Jonathan has a friend who lives in the mountains. He loves the sounds of nature abundantly surrounding his home. He abhors the sound of chain saws. He tenses and becomes irritated when he hears their buzzing and can often detect them many miles away. Their very sound brings visions of forest clear-cutting and other impositions upon the Earth Mother. The sound of chain saws are simply not in resonance with this man.

Recently this friend was helping build a tree house for his son. In the process it was necessary for a neighbor to use a chain saw to cut some dead trees limbs to use for the tree house. His neighbor put on noise-protecting headphones before he began. The chain saw buzzed away at a potentially deafening volume. The friend stood next to the chain saw, thinking happily about the tree house, knowing how pleased his son would be with it.

When the limbs had been cut, Jonathan's friend suddenly realized that he had not been adversely affected by the noise. It had not affected his hearing or his nervous system—there was no ringing in his ears, shortness of breath or tension usually experienced with even the distant sound of a chain saw. In fact, this man had actually enjoyed the sound despite the fact that he had been standing right next to it.

We cannot say that the next time this man hears a chain saw he will have the same experience. However, the conversion of an ordinarily noxious sound into a pleasant and helpful ally was transformative. It was a revelation of the possibility of altering the effects of sound through consciousness.

Certainly some frequencies might be hazardous to the human body and auric field. Studies show that some frequencies, when bombarding the nervous system of humans and animals, induce states of anxiety or fear and lower the immune response. But now we know that it's possible, though perhaps rare, to transform the effects of such sounds. When one learns to become fluid, anything can happen. Perception can change reality.

Voices of the Earth Mother

As you expand your consciousness of sound, remember that nature too can create sounds of immense magnitude. The great voice of the Earth Mother speaks deep and low during an earthquake. The thunder that follows lightning can be heard for miles.

Being at harmony with the Earth and one with nature can incorporate many different frequencies and purposes for these frequencies. The great circle of life, as some would call it, is a natural part of the Earth and its creatures. This includes sounds of birth and sounds of death. It seems that Mother Nature does not judge the parts of this cycle; from a cosmic perspective it is all one. One season is no better than another; spring (a time of birth) is not judged better than winter (a time of death). They are simply cycles, rhythms of life that have their purpose. As your prophets have said, "To every time there is a season and a purpose under heaven."

Humankind seems to have lost its awareness of harmony and oneness with nature. Without this awareness there is no harmony or balance. After winter comes spring. But when people pollute and destroy, they usually do not clean and rebuild what they destroy. A forest might be clear-cut to build apartment buildings. Thus humans create an extraordinary imbalance that usually does not occur in nature.

Sometimes your Earth Mother will create imbalances that make no sense to humankind—natural disasters like hurricanes, tornadoes and forest fires. But from a multidimensional view these disasters can be seen to be in ultimate harmony with the Earth and be part of the rhythms of nature. Human consciousness simply cannot understand this from its limited perspective.

Some theories of the creational process assert that chaos and disharmony exist before reorganization and reconstruction takes place. This is partly true. Some seemingly disharmonious sounds assist in shattering antiquated thought forms. For new forms to emerge, the old must collapse. We suggest that this disintegration is part of the natural process of creation and nothing to be feared, for it is part of the great circle. Some have great trepidations about "Earth changes." These changes have happened before and are part of the restoration of balance. Learning to shift your frequencies can help you learn to resonate with these changes, which are themselves aspects of the frequency-shifting phenomenon.

Ultimately all sounds can be understood as harmonious. But until you have mastered fluidity and the ability to transform sound, we suggest that you concentrate on creating only those sounds that are beneficial to yourself and the planet. Having lost the awareness of oneness with the planet for so long, humans need to restore the balance. Let the sounds you work with as well as the other frequencies you resonate with (nutritional, emotional or whatever) be in harmony with that of life, love and light. These are most helpful for your evolution at this time.

⦿   ⦿   ⦿

Chapter 18

Healing

What is healing? There is no simple answer. Healing means different things to different people. Its process also has multiple definitions. What, if any, is the connection between healing and frequency-shifting?

Sound Health

Your dictionaries often define health as "sound of body, mind and spirit." We like this definition because it uses the word "sound," and when incorporating its other meanings defines health as "the highest resonance of body, mind and spirit." Many believe that the process of healing is the restoration of this highest resonance to the body, mind and spirit. Considering that the basic principle of sound healing and vibrational medicine says that every organ, bone and system of the body has a specific resonant frequency, the concept of disease implies that a counterfrequency has encoded itself over the healthy one, causing part of the body to vibrate out of tune. With sound or other vibrational modalities it is possible to shift the frequency of the imbalanced part, enabling it to entrain to its normal frequency and reenter a state of health. From this perspective, healing and frequency-shifting would be synonymous, but this is not always the case from a traditional allopathic medical viewpoint.

The Allopathic Model

In the allopathic model of healing the body, mind and spirit are viewed as separate, as are the parts of the body. A metaphor often used for allopathic healing is that of plumbing: if there is a blocked drain, the blockage is removed; if there is a broken pipe, it is fixed. If a particular part of the body needs attention, then that part of the body receives

Sound Healers logo depicts the use of sound for healing. that attention, often without regard to anything else. We acknowledge the effectiveness of allopathic medicine. However, it does not acknowledge the interconnectedness of all things. To this form of healing the concept of frequency-shifting has no value. The concept of curing, however, fits well.

Curing, from our perspective, is the alleviation of the symptoms of an imbalance. Sometimes it also means the complete disappearance of the imbalance. Curing is not necessarily the same as healing or frequency-shifting.

The Holistic Model

In the holistic medical model the body, mind and spirit are seen to be connected. What affects any part of the body also affects the mind and the spirit. Many holistic healing modalities understand that ultimately all is vibration and that through shifting frequencies one can unblock energy and assist vibratory awakening through wellness.

Many holistic healing modalities such as chiropractic are concerned with releasing the innate intelligence within the body to reconnect with the universal intelligence that living creatures have. This is done by removing any interference with the life force. In chiropractic the energy is frequently cleared within the nervous system through manipulating the spine. In acupuncture it is done through placing needles at specific meridian points to free and balance the energy. Some holistic modalities use movement to clear energy, others use nutrition. Still others use sound, breath, sacred geometry, crystals or light.

Frequency Shifting As Healing

Regardless of the modality or tool, when one clears energy through releasing intelligence, one is actually shifting frequencies to effect a healing. In this holistic model true healing cannot occur unless the energy flow is clear and unimpeded. Healing is the result of shifting frequency because most imbalances are due to stuck energy. Energy is blocked because the part of the body (or mind or spirit) that is stuck is vibrating out of tune with its natural healthy resonance. By changing the vibrations, the energy often releases naturally and the imbalance disappears. We can learn to release this blocked energy and shift our own frequencies, thus healing ourselves.

From one perspective, all healing comes from within. But sometimes it is necessary to have some assistance from another person, one who can jump-start our vibratory field to help restore the natural flow of energy. As a healer friend says: "You can't tickle yourself, but another person can. It's the same thing with healing: Sometimes you need a secondary energy field to transfer energy and assist the healing process." We feel this has much validity. It is as though through resonance one person can assist the frequency shift of another and help restore the natural vibratory rate.

The healing process can be complicated. Sometimes it is like peeling the layers of an onion. Peel one layer and there is another; peel that layer and there is still another. Each layer reveals something different, and getting to the core of the problem can be difficult.

Placebo

There are many thought forms inherent in different holistic healing modalities. Because energy follows thought and manifestation follows energy, each healing thought form has validity and can manifest some level of success. Thus thoughts that are positive can have major effects. It is important for a healer to believe in the system being used. The allopathic modality too must be approached with confident for successful treatment. If medical doctors did not believe they had cures for conditions, there would be many fewer cures. Remember that the placebo effect (where patients are given sugar pills instead of drugs) has been shown to be over 70% effective in certain situations. The placebo effect reveals that a particular remedy is sometimes less important than the mind-body connection and demonstrates how powerful belief is.

In Tibetan medicine there is the understanding that healing is composed of three elements: the belief of the healer in the medicine; the belief of the person being healed in the healer; and the karma between the two. This is an interesting concept, and it implies there are some complications involved in the healing process.

As we said, when frequency shifts, imbalances can disappear. But this is not necessarily the focal point of using sound, geometry, crystals or other modalities that can shift frequency. When people focus primarily on curing a condition, their symptoms might disappear but they do not necessarily become more conscious beings. When focus is limited to a cure, only temporary relief might be achieved when a condition disappears. Not infrequently the condition returns because its actual cause or source has not been addressed.

Addressing the cause of an imbalanced condition is essential. When individuals do this, they often change their lifestyles. This demonstrates healing as frequency-shifting. For example, if a person has a nail in his shoe, he might put a bandage on his foot. This will help temporarily, but sooner or later the nail will wear through and the problem will return. Another bandage might help, but until the individual realizes the nail is there and removes it (or somehow deals with the actual source instead of the symptom), healing will usually be temporary.

We say "usually" because spirit is extraordinary, and sometimes true healings can occur in the most unique ways. It is possible for a healer to put a bandage on a foot and have the nail disappear, never to return. Healing energies are remarkable and diverse. Anything is possible. We merely suggest that healings are most effective when the nail is found and removed from the shoe.

Expanding Consciousness

A primary purpose for frequency-shifting involves expanding consciousness. We acknowledge the importance of aligning and balancing that which is out of alignment, but the frequency shift does not end there. It continues with the activation and expansion of the individual's consciousness, which then often prompts him to alter his lifestyle and life's work. As the person's awareness is expanded he begins to understand his connection to others, to the planet and to the all.

The idea of "cure" implies that something is wrong or that

a condition needs to be corrected. This is certainly a constricting thought form, though a prevalent one. This belief blames the individual who has the condition because something "should" be better.

But conditions often manifest to teach the individual something. Humans can choose imbalances in order to learn and grow, perhaps not on a conscious level but on a soul level. Sometimes a condition will not leave until the individual has learned the needed lesson. Frequently the lesson is about changing beliefs and patterns that have been encoded at a deep, even cellular level. Changing one's consciousness through shifting frequency can greatly assist this learning process.

Frequency-shifting implies that changing your vibrational rate will assist you toward health and wellness. But that goal is not necessarily the focal point or even the main purpose for learning to shift your frequency. The purpose, from our perspective, is to become more awake, more conscious, more divine. It is not simply to heal an imbalanced condition, but to realize that in divinity all is whole.

From our perspective, the critical point of shifting frequency is for people to wake up, to understand their part in the galactic activation occurring on this planet and to assist and work with each other. Shifting frequencies means being able to encode more light and love into ourselves, from our DNA to our subtle bodies. It means being more compassionate and loving to both self and others. This is the tremendous leap in consciousness that the saints, masters and avatars have been teaching for eons. That is what shifting frequencies is really about.

Encoding Light and Love

Encoding more light and love into oneself will frequently trigger a healing, but if not, that is fine. What an individual does with himself, his thoughts and actions is what is most important. It will not really matter whether one has an imbalance or a condition when one practices kindness and love, which anyone can do. Although it would be easier to practice kindness and love in a state of physical health, there is no guarantee that health brings more compassion.

Physical health does not mean one is in balance and alignment with the energies of the universe. It is not necessary for light, love and higher consciousness. Conversely, having an imbalanced condition does not mean that one is out of alignment with the universe.

There are too many on planet Earth in good physical health who have little or no regard for the energy of love. These beings might be in physical alignment (at least temporarily), but they might be extremely out of balance with other aspects of themselves, with others and with the planet. They might be in a state of physical health, but it would be useful for them to learn to shift their frequencies to become truly whole and balanced and assist others and the planet.

If your purpose for reading, then working with the ideas in these discussions is primarily for curing, that is noble and good. We send our blessing and trust that you will be successful. We also trust that you will take your work a step further, using these ideas to enhance consciousness and encode more light and love into yourself. Then you will use your frequency shifts for the betterment not only of yourself and others, but of the planet as well. We thank you for your work.

🌀　　　🌀　　　🌀

Chapter 19

The Language of Light Part 1

There is a language of light. It is encoded into each and every cell of your being. It is encoded into the very fiber and matrix of reality. It is in fact reality as it can be known from your consciousness. The language of light is not an Earth language as you know it, although its elements have been picked up by some of your ancestors and utilized in several different Earth languages. These are the mother tongue of your planet.

The language of light is an aspect of the Creator. When the "Word" was spoken, it was in reality this language of light. From the Word, the primordial vibrations (note that we say vibrations) were sent out to the different universes and planes of existence that were to be. From this language of light these different universes, planes of existence and everything inherent in them came to be.

The language of light is not merely a physical sound, nor is it a physical form. It is neither, yet it is both, for it is much more. The language of light ultimately manifested as the physical plane. Inherent in this plane, in its beings and its sounds, is an aspect of the language of light. These vibrations were manifested directly from the Creator at the begin-

ning. This language of light was the Creator-being express-
ing Itself in order to know Itself. The vibrations filtered
down through the different dimensions, universes and realities of being. On each different plane of existence it took
shape and form. These shapes and forms and their vibratory level were unique to their plane.

The language of light is a composite of frequencies that
represents all that has ever been or ever will be. It is found
within your chants, tones and sacred mantras. Fragments of
it are also found within your common languages because
aspects of it are found within all sounds. In previous discussions we have spoken of sound as being the original manifesting principle and of how everything is composed of
sound. These sounds are the language of light.

All vibratory beings, sentient and nonsentient, are composed of these vibrations. Your rocks, trees and elements all
sing this language of light, and very purely so, for they are
naturally aspects of the Creator. Your cars, computers and
home furnishings sing aspects of this language, as do your
clothing, buildings and whatnot. Everything that is, is an
aspect of the Creator and therefore everything that is, is an
aspect of this language of light. You yourself are composed
of this language, just as you are an aspect of the Creator.

If you could see beyond the veils of illusion into the depths
of the creational form, you would see that all is composed of
this language of light. Imagine that you had a special device
with a lens that could look beyond the dimensional gateways
into the very fiber of the different realities. You would see
that the fibers of these realities were composed of this language of light. If you had a very special speaker, you could
also hear this language as it was originally created.

What does it look like? How does it sound? You would
be surprised, because both the form and the vibration of this
language of light might seem strangely familiar. It would be

familiar because before you came to this planet it was spoken in your dream places. It was, in fact, the very essences of those places, for the very fibers of the different realities encompass them, too.

This language of light has many forms and these forms have sounds—they are in fact sounds. The two are one. The sound creates the form and the form creates the sound. The world of duality has twofoldedness. Unity has only singularity—the language of light.

If you were to look at this language of light in its causative form, you would recognize in it many of the letters of the Earth's sacred languages. In the highest dimensional levels, these letters are personified as living beings—enormous, glorious beings of light. From certain perspectives they are seen as straight lines that meet and form interference patterns. On other levels they are perceived as straight lines that curve below. These beings meet together and nest, forming what look like lines that interpenetrate each other at different angles, creating a multitude of different patterns.

For those who perceive them, these lines spin, creating shapes within themselves as they meet, and their meetings create further configurations. In the forming patterns you can see the movement of the electrons around the atoms and the atoms themselves. If you were to look at the planets and the stars and track their movement over the months, years and eons, you would see these patterns manifesting as the language of light. These different lines were directly known by the ancient seers and were incorporated in the sacred alphabets of the sacred languages on Earth.

In your ancient traditions, this language of light is understood to be the primary creative force. We have already referred to it as the Word which was in the "beginning." The Jewish mystics understood this when their Lord said, "Let there be light," for it was this language that created light. At the very creational level this energy was, first and foremost, light. And when this light illuminated, both the darkness and the void became filled. This light brought light and life. It also created all that existed, from the planets to the quarks. These all filtered down from the Creator as aspects of the language of light.

Hebrew was understood by these ancient Jewish mystics to be a divinely created language. It was called a "fire" language, delivered by the Divine unto humankind. The different letters were believed to make up the building blocks of reality. In the Jewish tradition each sacred letter represented an energy, a sound, a form, an essence. The letters were alive—a living aspect of the Creator. From the perspective of these mystics, the language of light was Hebrew.

Did you know that you are part of this language? Yes, everything is. If you could listen closely enough or see deeply enough, you would see and hear that the very fiber of your being sings this language of light and is this language of light. It is the energy that makes up the electron moving around the atom that moves around the molecule. It is also the molecule itself, for it sings differently depending on what is being sounded.

In the Hindu tradition the creator God is called Brahman. In that tradition there is the expression "Nada Brahman." It refers to the creator God being sound. Nada Brahman: sound is God. God is sound. Brahman, the creator God, manifested Saraswati, his consort. Through the lips of Saraswati come the ancient bija mantras, which the Hindu mystics understood to be the building blocks of reality. To these Hindu mystics, the language of light was Sanskrit.

The word *bija* means "seed." These sounds make up the letters of the Sanskrit alphabet. In Hindu thought, the bijas seeded the very nature of reality. Many of you may have seen Hindu artwork depicting the chakras of the body. The chakras look like flowers (they are said to be lotuses). On the petals of the flower of each chakra are Sanskrit figures—letters of this sacred alphabet. These are the bija mantras, which are said to make up the actual essence of the chakra. Each spinning petal is actually the energy vortex created by these bijas sounding together.

The tetragrammaton, the four letters of the Hebrew alphabet regarded as the divine name of God, arranged to produce a human-like figure.

There are many sacred alphabets composing the language of light. Sanskrit is one, so is ancient Hebrew, and there are others as well. The ancient Egyptian God Thoth would think a word, speak its name and bring it into being. This being spoke ancient Egyptian—also a sacred language and an aspect of the language of light. Tibetan and Chinese are also said to be of this language. All Earth's languages and dialects have aspects of this language of light, although many modern languages are creations from other languages and these are creations from still other languages. Your modern English has been bounced around so many times, it is amazing that you have any aspects left from one of the original sacred languages. But of course, there are.

Would you like an example of a pure aspect of the language of light? The word "ma" (or we should more properly say, the sound): Think about it—this word is found in every language and it always connotes femininity and motherhood. It is a sound uttered by infants everywhere: "Maaaaa!" Even before there is conscious awareness of the meaning of the word, *ma* is constantly being sounded. *Ma* is a sound and word from the language of light. Feel its power!

From your perspective, you may wonder why, if *ma* is a sound from the language of light, it is not even more powerful. Why does the sound not border upon the miraculous? Why isn't light created when it is spoken? Why do things not manifest when it is voiced?

We would suggest a number of possibilities: First, in terms of the physical plane, ordinary speech is a stepped-down form of sound energy. As an aspect of the Creator, sacred sound has traveled through many dimensional levels in order to manifest upon the Earth. It has been transduced multitudinous times. It is, to state the obvious, the lowest of common denominators in terms of sound, since it is very third-dimensional. It is the grossest level of sound that has manifested, and it needs to be, since it is acoustic and audible. In order to manifest to humans on the physical plane, sound waves must travel between 16 and 20 thousand times a second, the level of human hearing. This is quite slow compared to other forms of energy, which can vibrate to trillions of times per second, such as the phenomenon you call light.

Yet this gross sound

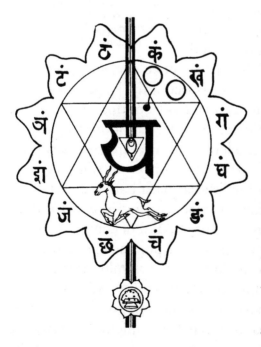

The heart chakra with bija mantras in the petals.

does the trick. It travels between the mouth and ear of those using it and conveys information. This is quite marvelous! Have you thought how incredible it is that you can communicate with words? It is a remarkable thing that with one word you can project understanding of an object or a mood or a desire. In your mystical traditions the naming of an object gave the namer incredible ability with the named object. This was a gift given to Adam, the first man from your Old Testament. It is a gift that humankind still possesses.

This is the power inherent in just one word. If you put several words together, the information exchange can be quite enormous. What a gift language of any sort is to the consciousness of the user! Think about the sound *ma*. Think of the feelings and pictures—the emotions and memories that you can create simply by repeating this word a few times.

Your words have extraordinary power, yet most are not aware of this power. What would happen if you gained the ability to actually manifest in the physical reality by using your voice? Think of that power—and the responsibility you would have!

🌀　　🌀　　🌀

Chapter 20

The Language of Light Part II

We continue our discussion of the language of light. To repeat briefly, this language was the original sound of the Creator and has been known in different traditions as the Word or the "sound current." Its elements have remained in virtually every language. In particular, sacred languages such as Hebrew and Sanskrit maintain a pure encodement of the language of light. As it filtered down through the higher dimensions, it became physical sound and speech. We noted that the sound *Ma* is actually a fragment of this language of light and asked you to reflect on the power inherent in that sound. We asked you to consider what would happen if you could actually manifest on the physical plane through speech.

You cannot at your present development create physical-plane manifestations through sound. You can say "car" and others will know what you mean. If you are waiting outside a restaurant with a ticket and a valet nearby, the odds are that the word "car" will cause your vehicle to be delivered to you curbside. However, you are not at the point where your vehicle would miraculously materialize next to you just by saying the word. And you should be grateful that this is so, for as a species you are not yet ready for this gift. You would probably have destroyed yourself eons ago if you had had this ability.

These sacred languages that stem from the original language of light are "guarded" languages, inasmuch as there are extraordinary beings associated with these languages who guard them against misuse. Otherwise, as we have inferred, your average human might attempt to use them unwisely.

Think for a moment about all the pain and suffering that can be inflicted solely through words. Harsh words spoken in anger or fear can truly demoralize another person. What would happen if humans could use sound from that greater level of manifestation without the consciousness necessary for such control? This is why the language of light is guarded. Only those who have achieved the level of required consciousness may successfully use it.

Etheric-plane manifestations frequently occur with some of your more seasoned practitioners of the spirit. These beings work with the energy of love and are allowed to use the language of light for the good of all. Sometimes there are even physical manifestations that result from the conscious use of the language. Those attuned to sacred sound can create many amazing manifestations. Thankfully, they have the consciousness to use such a gift.

One of the missing concepts in terms of manifesting with sound is the knowledge that there is this language of light. This ignorance has helped lessen the impact of any of the mother tongues in terms of their ability to create. When these languages were used exclusively as sacred languages, they had much more power. They were used for chanting and prayers to communicate and praise the Divine. Their extraordinary power became diluted more and more as the language began to be used for ordinary conversation and communication. Many of the languages remaining on the Earth that are used for common speech are mere shadows of what they once were.

Also missing is the ability of humans to visualize the meaning and intention of these sounds. For most it is a lost art/science. Coupling human consciousness with (or on) a vibration can be extremely powerful. It creates a stepping-up of the vibratory response of language to another level. We are not merely describing the ability to "see" something while you are sounding; what we are describing is the projection of embodied consciousness onto the sound. It is quite complex, yet very simple.

As a precaution, certain safety mechanisms are built into using of sound for manifestation. These come from the guardians of the language of light to ensure that the language is not misused. In order to properly utilize the language, you must first pass through a gateway to fully understand the principle and practice. One begins the journey through that gateway by learning to love and to project love onto the sound. It is that easy.

Most of your sacred mantras from your different traditions embody this principle and practice. Your *Om* sound is one of the purest examples. The Hindu tradition believes that this was the primordial sound from which other sounds emerged. If you would like to understand this, simply begin by humming "mmmm" with your mouth closed. Then very slowly open your mouth, rounding your lips into an "oh" sound. If you can, try to nasalize this sound near its completion so that it travels into the sinus region and above. Then slowly begin to bring the sound down again into the mouth, gradually closing the mouth until it again sounds like "mmmm."

If you try this sound a few times and focus your attention and hearing on it, you may hear or sense a spectrum of sound within that one sound. Many different sounds make up the *Om;* it is an amazing thing to explore. It will resonate your body and your head, your etheric fields and bodies. It is quite balancing by itself even without any visualization.

Om has many meanings, including, of course, peace and love. It is a multidimensional word, for its meaning operates on many different levels. One level is an aspect of the Hindu trinity, which incorporates Brahman the creator, Vishnu the preserver and Shiva the destroyer. It is much more than this, but we mention this in order to describe what multidimensional sound is all about.

The language of light is, of course, multidimensional sound. When such a language incorporates on the physical plane (we know no other way to describe it) and when it has maintained enough of its integrity to manifest as part of a language system on Earth, it is a powerful sound. Many different traditions have chants that incorporate sacred languages, or at least large portions of original sacred languages.

We have named some languages as being of the mother tongue, but we do not wish to cite all the specific languages that came directly from the language of light, for we do not wish to inadvertently miss one and offend someone. We would like to suggest that there are a few "primitive" languages that are seldom recognized as sacred (ask your indigenous or aboriginal peoples if they believe their language was divinely created). We also suggest that some of the sacred languages from the language of light have not survived (does anyone speak ancient Egyptian anymore?) and are no longer remembered.

You humans frequently get very possessive about language. Some years ago Jonathan was with a master of sound from

India who was a devotee of Saraswati. Now, as you may
remember, Sanskrit is understood by Hindus to be a sacred
language, a creational language. It is, to its believers, the
original language, and that is that! Jonathan and his friend
from India looked at a copy of a major international weekly
magazine. There on the front cover was a story about the
origin of language. A primary "mother" language had been
discovered and traced to somewhere in Europe. Jonathan's
friend found the story amusing and a little disappointing.
Sanskrit was obviously the original language; the article was
obviously wrong.

And it *was* wrong, but not because Sanskrit was the original language of the gods—the language of light—because
several guarded languages have come down from the other
planes as aspects of the language of light. Hebrew, yes!
Tibetan, yes! And more.

Different planes and thought forms manifest and are manifested from specific sacred languages (once again, at this
level there is no difference between the thing and what it
does—its sound). Sometimes these sacred languages merge
and create reality bases together.

There is a new language of light that seems to be emerg-
ing on the planet at this time. Many are now beginning to
tune in to it. Some are able to tone it, some are gifted
enough to draw it. For some it is a new language they speak,
for others an ancient language they remember. Sometimes it
sounds like gibberish or a composite of Sanskrit and Hebrew
with something else thrown in. Sometimes it is composed
entirely of harmonics. Sometimes it seems like an ancient,
forgotten alphabet. Sometimes it looks like geometries.

For some, this language is the speech of the angels,
extraterrrestials or gods and goddesses. For many it is
uncontrollable. For still others it is incomplete. Sometimes
it is a spoken language we can understand when we hear it

from a world we do not know. At other times it is comprehensible only to the speaker. We suggest that this language, as always, is only an aspect of the language of light. It represents the operating of consciousness at a level more advanced than the purely communicative level. And it accesses a level of a much higher dimensionality than normally used by humans.

This new language conveys communication, but frequently it operates at a plane in which creation can begin to be experienced. At times this new language can interface and affect reality and the creation of the physical, which was also true of your more ancient sacred languages. You might have healings and regenerations, for it resonates downward to the cellular level. It can create change and frequency shifts of unimaginable proportions.

We would like to acknowledge that tone, timbre and pitch all operate out of this language of light. Harmonics and the frequency of the sound are all aspects of this language. It depends on the person who is creating it and the person receiving it. For some, this language is purely tonal and for others it sounds like speech. How can this be?

There is a shape created from the *Om* sound that can be seen by meditators. Its geometric visualization, the sri yantra, which the ancient rishis in India saw and drew, looks like overlapping triangles within a circle. It is thousands of years old and can be found in numerous Hindu temples. Some years ago this shape was duplicated in a laboratory when someone chanted *Om* into a machine that

displayed form from sound [see *Cymatics* video by Hans Jenny]. It was the same shape the rishis saw! The "O" created the circle, the "mmmm" the overlapping triangles. Quite revelatory.

Some have seen the bija mantra for the *Om* at the area of the third eye when chanting the sound, which looks a bit like the number 3 with a squiggly line above it. These curved lines are seen instead of the sri yantra. Same sound, different sacred shape, because it is a different level of reality one is accessing. This demonstrates the vibrational level that the chanter and the receiver are operating from. The vibrational level and perspective of the language of that level can be very different from one time to another. Despite how it may be seen or heard, remember that all aspects of the language originate from the original language of light of the Creator. There are many different aspects, many different sounds and forms yet all come from the One.

Open your eyes, your ears, your minds and your hearts— indeed, open your spirit — to begin to perceive the language of light and allow it to unfold for you. Regardless of the level from which it is perceived, the understanding and experience of the language of light as an aspect of the Creator Source can be a valuable tool for expanding consciousness and shifting frequency.

🌀　　🌀　　🌀

Chapter 21

The Angel Chakra

In our last two chapters we focused on the language of light. This language, the breath of the Divine, is the original vibrational essence from whence all creation sprang. Several ancestral languages, such as Hebrew and Sanskrit, are closely aligned to this original mother tongue of God. In the Hindu tradition the original seven chakras were said to be composed of aspects of this language, and Hindu bija mantras, which make up the Sanskrit alphabet, are ascribed to specific chakras.

Mantras and other primordial sounds, such as the vowel sounds, can open, balance and align the chakras. In this discussion we will focus on a new chakra coming on line—one we call the angel chakra—and how a particular sound from the language of light works to activate it. We will also bring in the teachings of some special guests.

The word *chakra* is a Sanskrit term meaning wheel, because chakras are seen as spinning wheels of light by those who can see subtle energies. In most traditions there are seven main chakras, which are transduction points, places where subtle energy from other planes begins to densify or, if you will, the place where thought begins to manifest as

VOWEL	CHAKRA	BIJA
EEE	CROWN	OM
AY	THIRD EYE	SHAM
EYE	THROAT	HAM
AH	HEART	YAM
OH	NAVEL	RAM
OOO	SACRAL	VAM
UH	BASE	LAM

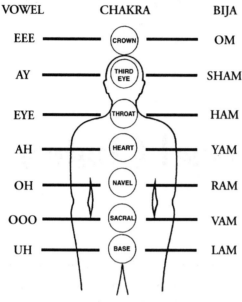

The Sacred Vowel/Bija Mantra System

matter. We are not saying that chakras are third-dimensional, but that they are perceptible from a third-dimensional point of view. Many people are able to see them; still more are able to feel them. Scientific instrumentation is even beginning to record and validate the chakras as a real phenomenon. (We note the humor: Until your instruments can validate them, registering electromagnetics or whatnot, your hard-core thinkers refuse to acknowledge chakras despite their presence in different traditions for thousands of years.)

The energy from chakras densifies as it comes down into your bodies, becoming your acupuncture points and meridians, finally transducing into the physical body itself. Imbalances in the physical body can be detected through the chakras. Frequently, healers who work with subtle energy can detect imbalances before they manifest in the physical body by sensing imbalances in the chakras.

Through balancing the chakras, imbalances in the physical body will often disappear. There is a feedback loop occurring with this energy. The physical body interfaces with the energy of the chakras and vice versa. Most of the time an imbalance will manifest first in a chakra, then later in the physical body. It is possible, through a traumatic injury, for example, for both the physical body and the chakras to be simultaneously imbalanced. Healing the physical occurs much more rapidly when the subtle anatomy—particularly the chakras—are realigned after physical trauma. Hopefully, medical professionals will begin to understand this and include treatment of the subtle anatomy in conjunction with the physical.

There are seven main chakras, seven spinning balls of energy, located centrally in the front and the posterior of the body. As we briefly describe these seven chakras, we will describe sounds that are useful for resonating and balancing these areas. If you are interested in trying these sounds, we suggest that you work with either the sacred vowel sounds or the bija mantras at first. Make each of these sounds a minimum of three and a maximum of nine times to resonate each chakra. As you progress, begin to combine them, using both sacred vowels and bijas. Create the sound in a gentle and relaxed voice; do not strain yourself. You will be amazed how little effort is required to create a sound that can shift your frequencies.

Sounds That Balance Each Chakra

The first chakra, located at the bottom of the trunk, is involved with the physical process of elimination. It is a chakra associated with the energy of survival and with grounding to the physical plane. To balance this chakra with a sacred vowel, make the very deepest *uh* (as in cup) sound that you can and focus your intention on this area. A bija mantra that resonates this area is *lam*.

The second chakra, about three inches below your navel, is associated with sexual energy and with much of the life force. The sexual energy is a divine energy, but has been the source of much confusion and abuse in your society. It manifests as deep emotional issues. Remember that this chakra is not better or worse than any other chakra; it is simply a conduit for a particular aspect of energy. To sound this chakra with a sacred vowel, make a higher-pitched *oo* (as in you) sound while focusing your intention on this area. A bija mantra that resonates this chakra is *yam*.

The third chakra, at the navel and a little above, is the solar plexus chakra. Its energy is associated with the organs of digestion and also with power. Many people in business and politics work with this chakra, sometimes seeming to exclude all other chakras in their focus. To sound this chakra with a sacred vowel, make a higher-pitched *oh* (as in go) sound while focusing intention on this area. A bija mantra to resonate this chakra is *ram*.

The fourth chakra, in the center of the chest between the nipples, is the heart center. On the physical, it works with the lungs and the heart. On the emotional, it works with the energy of compassion and love. This is a most important chakra to open for those working with the energy of healing. Its balance and alignment can be an extraordinary gift. To sound this chakra with a sacred vowel make a higher-pitched *ah* sound while focusing your intention there. A bija mantra for this chakra is *yam*.

The fifth chakra is at the throat, above the base of the neck. It is associated with communication as well as the ears, sense of hearing and the vocal apparatus. To sound this chakra with a sacred vowel, make a higher-pitched *eye* (as in my) sound while focusing your intention on it. A bija mantra to resonate this chakra is *ham*.

The sixth chakra, in the center of the forehead above the eyes, is often called the third eye or brow chakra. It is associated with inner and visionary seeing mental activity and other brain functions. In many psychics this chakra is very well developed. To sound the brow chakra, make a higher-pitched *ay* (as in the word say) sound while focusing your intention on this area. A bija mantra for this chakra is *sham.*

The seventh chakra, at the top of the head, is called the crown chakra. It is associated with the induction of spiritual energy into the body and certain higher brain functions. This chakra is normally not fully open in most humans, though pictures of saints and other spiritual beings with halos are depictions of activated crown chakras. To sound the crown, make the highest pitched *eeee* (as in the word me) sound that you can make while focusing your intention there. A bija mantra for this chakra is *om.*

These are the seven major chakras found in the various traditions. For those interested in further experiences with sound and these seven chakras, Jonathan has recently completed a recording, *The Chakra Chant,* that features the sacred vowel sounds and bija mantras using special Pythagorean tunings in conjunction with environmental and elemental sounds

As humans progress on their evolutionary path, other dormant chakras are coming on line. They are being activated to help raise the vibrations of the individual to assist personal and planetary activation. Some new chakras that have been described by others include the thymus chakra, associated with the Christ energy and located between the heart chakra and the throat chakra; and the "alta major," associated with channeling, found at the back of the head directly below the occipital region. Many are becoming aware of other chakras that exist below and above the body at transpersonal points.

The Angel Chakra

A new chakra has been activated that Jonathan calls the *angel chakra.* It is located between the third eye and the crown at the area called the fontanel, the place on the skull that remains soft on a newborn infant. The purpose of this chakra is to bring more light into the subtle and physical bodies. Its activation also connects individuals with spirit guides, or guardian angels. The angel chakra is also associated with higher activities of the brain and with accessing different frequencies of consciousness through tuning the brain.

Jonathan's initial conscious contact with this chakra began in the Mayan ruin of Palenque in Mexico, where he had gone for the Harmonic Convergence in 1987. As related in *Healing Sounds,* Jonathan sounded a harmonic, and suddenly the room became partially illuminated. So many different initiatory experiences had occurred during that time that after this sound-into-light phenomenon (along with the half dozen friends in the room), he merely acknowledged it to everyone else and then dismissed it.

Months later when Jonathan came upon a reference to the ancient mystery schools giving initiations in total darkness (the initiate had to create his own light), he focused on the experience in Mexico. He knew it had to do with some kind of activation of the pineal gland through sound, perhaps the release of specific neurochemicals activated by specific harmonics. In *Healing Sounds* he speculated that melatonin is produced to assist this sound-into-light phenomenon. Recently a scientist has actually proved that melatonin is released through self-created sound, adding third-dimensional validity to the theory.

During his teachings of vocal harmonics, Jonathan would present a specific visualization to his students while they made a particular harmonic phoneme: *nurr,* an Eastern word for light. When sounded in a particular manner, *nurr* can produce very powerful harmonics that resonate the brain. (*Nurr,* incidentally, is the sound Jonathan used in Palenque.)

His students made this sound and visualized it going from the roof of the mouth up through the sinus cavities and into the brain, where it stimulated the pineal area. Jonathan found that he could feel energy being generated in the heads of his students while they created this sound and visualization. Students would see light or geometric forms during this experience. Some would get in touch with spirit guides. Many who experienced this activation felt a shaft of light enter the upper portion of their heads and travel into the heart, illuminating that area with a glorious radiance.

Jonathan knew an important activation was occurring. Initially, he thought this sound was activating the third eye. However, the energy was actually coming from an area about three inches above the third eye, at the point of the fontanel, but he did not consciously realize this until last fall.

During a particular workshop Jonathan was at the part of his teaching when his students tone the sound *nurr* while doing the visualization. As usual, he walked around, passing his hand over the foreheads of the students. This time, however, he realized that it was not the third eye being activated, but something else. He silently asked, "What's going on?" A voice (we will let you guess whose it was) told him: "You are always talking about new chakras coming on line. What do you think you are doing?"

At the end of the workshop Jonathan was quite bewildered. This was obviously a new chakra being activated, but what was it? What would it be called? What was its purpose? What activation was occurring? Looking for answers, Jonathan spoke with many of his colleagues. Some recalled that there might have been a name for this area in some obscure spiritual text, but no one could remember what it was. And no one could tell him what the purpose of this chakra was.

We conferred with Jonathan about this new chakra activation, telling him that it was to be called the angel chakra. Because the activation of this chakra was multidimensional, it involved many things, including the embodiment of more light into the individual and the opening of higher levels of consciousness and communication. However, despite inner guidance and information, Jonathan frequently seeks validation through other sources. This occurred after our first contact with each other, for he would not even acknowledge our existence until he was given a book in which we were named and described!

Such is the case with the angel chakra. He went to two of his favorite humans, who channel wondrous entities. He asked them about this new chakra and then recorded their responses. We are pleased to present this information to you.

The first material came from Shadonai, a glorious interdimensional entity channeled through Karen Anderson.

Message from Shadonai

There are many, many chakras. Each one of them is valuable and serves several different purposes. One area that's particularly chakra-rich and fascinating is between the third eye and the crown. Chakras in this area serve the ultimate purpose of blending into the crown.

This area you have been asked to work with has to do with light. It is associated with the inpouring of spirit into the body, with the encodement of more light into the body. This is the last area that closes in humans as they become embodied souls, even after the crown and the third eye are closed. This happens with souls or babies or entities after they are born and is known as the soft spot or fontanel.

For some entities, beautiful entities, this area never closes. It is the light that is flowing in and the light that is flowing out. If the being is of sufficient evolution, a beautiful light of rainbow and textured colors flows out— Mother Teresa was an example of this. It could be found in her skull that there were areas where the bones did not close, for her light was such that she carried the light of the world within her, and it came out of her into the planet, creating a halo over her. Such is the case with other beings who are taking teachings from other galaxies, from the Solar Logos, from different entities. They are keeping this energy center open and using this chakra to pull in energy from these different levels, which guides them in their intricate and interesting work.

Certain souls and all babies are given instructions for this lifetime after they have landed here. In a way this encodement is sent down in light through their guardian angels, through the fontanel into that area, so the souls can remember their true purpose after the shock of being embodied in the density of matter. Sometimes it is very difficult to remember, "Oh yes! I wanted to finish such and such or continue my pursuit of music"— or art or government or sports or whatever it was the soul wanted to do in this lifetime. Instruction can be sent in through the fontanel to the soul once it has embodied. This is why it is the last area to be closed. It is an essential contact point, the angelic point, the point of light.

Again, the primary function of this chakra is the encodement of more light into the body, the inpouring of spirit. One minor function is to resonate the frontal lobes and other portions of the brain. We can begin to expand our cerebral capacity as intelligence increases and multidimensional connections occur. Ultimately, we will use 100 percent of the brain on our evolutionary march to higher consciousness.

You use the sound *nurr* in this activation? *Nurr* is an ancient sound from one of the guarded alphabets. They have giant gates, as the gates of heaven were once described, gates of the holy alphabets in many dimensions that are guarded by vast, incredible angelic beings with swords of truth. Certain information has been released down through time from these holy alphabets. One sound released is the sound *nurr*. The word *nurr* has been translated into some of the Earth languages as the word for light. It is an actual multidimensional embodiment of light because it is a sacred being or entity who has chosen to send part of its vibration down to this level. It is a very beautiful sound to work with for this purpose.

You have been given instructions to empower or initiate people by giving teachings and working with this area. This is because this area is known as a light-based center and you work with the angels of light and sound. We conclude by saying congratulations on being given such an assignment.

We thank Shadonai for this fine information on the angel chakra. Jonathan could not truly hear or accept this material through his own personal channel, so we appreciate the assistance of others in this task.

Still wishing additional information and verification of the angel chakra, he went to another gifted being named Kay Mora, who channels a collective known as Wings of Song. This information came through the entity Christina of that group.

Christina of the Wings of Song

This angel chakra is a new chakra that has come into being in relation to the changes going on on the Earth level, particularly the need for more sensitivity and more direction. It allows more direct communication with the guides and all the deeper wisdoms. The communication of this particular chakra is one of a guide, which is not the same chakra used by those who seek to communicate with people. It is a more personal direction for the individual, meant only for the individual and guided for the individual. It is not information for the individual to share with others for their lives. It is only for the life of that particular individual and the things that fit within the framework of that life. It is the only direct communication for the individual in his life. Wherever it is needed, it is received. It is personal, not universal. It is important for one's heart to be truly open to interpret this information clearly.

This information from Christina offered an additional perspective of the angel chakra that Jonathan found useful. We trust that the contributions of Shadonai and Christina have resonated with you also. We have no doubt that as awareness of this chakra grows, many of you will find yourselves becoming conscious of this chakra and will receive new understandings about it. In conclusion, we will summa-

rize information about the angel chakra to assist your understanding.

Summary

The angel chakra is an energy center in the head between
the third eye and crown. Located at the fontanel, the soft
spot on a baby's head, it is a center associated with the
inpouring of spirit and light into the body. This light may
be perceived as both energy and information, thus the angel
chakra is a center where the guidance of spirits or angels may
be accessed. The information accessed here pertains to an
individual's true purpose in embodying on this planet. This
chakra works with higher brain functions, in particular, the
frontal lobes. Activating the angel chakra can increase the
ability of the individual to use more of his or her brain for
multidimensional consciousness—telepathy and seemingly
miraculous abilities such as manifesting thought into matter.

The angel chakra can be activated using the *nurr* sound
with specific visualizations. There are other ways it can be
activated; in fact, for many people it has been involved in
healing and higher consciousness. We suggest, however, that
this activation will occur only when an individual is ready.
The awareness of the angel chakra is important to those
working with frequency-shifting. Its activation brings more
light into your being and helps access communication with
higher levels of consciousness. As more of you begin to work
with the angel chakra, you will receive further assistance in
both personal and planetary frequency shifts.

⟨ℳ⟩　　　⟨ℳ⟩　　　⟨ℳ⟩

Afterword

We unite once again for this one final message. There is always more to say, and we trust that in future writings we will continue to illuminate and entertain you with our words.

We have attempted in these few pages to put forth some ideas and exercises that might be useful to you in your continued evolution on this and other planets and planes. We trust that this material will assist you in your development. If nothing else, we hope it has helped encode certain ideas that may have been dormant in your psyche. Maybe you have had a few "aha's" and perhaps a few "oh no's" as well. This is good. It is our mutual belief that in the fluid nature of reality you must momentarily embrace those thoughts you are resonant with and discard the others for the moment. Frequently on your Earth plane you either totally embrace a reality base offered by another or totally discard it. It is perhaps best to use discernment. Do not believe all of anyone's truth if one aspect strikes home, nor dismiss it entirely because something seems amiss. You have your expression of not "throwing out the baby with the bath water." We suggest you remember the wisdom of this.

Dear reader friends, we ask two things of you. First, while everything in the universe is in a state of vibration, including the words on these pages and the pages themselves, we suggest that the best way to begin to embody any of the material in this book is to work with sound yourself. Learning to affect and influence your vibratory resonance, indeed to shift your frequencies with sound, is not only extremely powerful but also fun. It is quite enjoyable as well as highly transformational. Make sound for yourself. When possible, make sound with others. If necessary, study with a teacher, but always remember to be in a state of joyfulness whenever you can. Solemnnity and sacredness are not the same. Do not confuse the two. Frequently they are opposites. You can be sacred and at the same time be quite happy. Remember, in your Bible it says to "make a joyful noise" unto the Divine. Many times, by the very nature of sounding, you will become joyous even if you were not at its start. So be open to being joyful! And be in sound.

Second, we suggest the importance of being in sound together with others. To sound with another creates a synergistic effect where the sum of the parts is greater than the whole. When sounding in a group, the synergistic effect is quite extraordinary. It is magnificent. And it is real. You don't have to sound "good" to do this. You merely have to be willing to experiment with the experience of making sacred sound together. Ultimately, this simply means to make any sounds together. As you do this, through the forces of life, the universe and resonance, you will undoubtedly start to entrain with each other, vibrate together and all manner of wonderful things will happen. You may share a group mind. You may soul-travel together. You may create mutual realities together. But foremost, we assure you, you will have fun—and you will be *divine*—and that is all that matters.

In the future we will discuss more aspects of frequency-shifting such as aromatherapy, movement, nutrition and other modalities, as well as further information on the areas discussed in these pages. There will always be more, and we give thanks for that. For now, however, we feel that there is sufficient material in these pages that is useful. These are very interesting times. Knowledge of shifting frequencies is important for everyone interested in personal and planetary activation.

Remember always to work with the energies of love in whatever technique, exercise or modality you are working with. It has been suggested that love is the glue that holds the universe together. We agree. Be in love. Be in light. Be in sound. You are remarkable beings, and your purpose on this and other planets and dimensions is only beginning to make itself known. Enjoy!

— *Jonathan Goldman and Shamael*

Bibliography

Abraham, Ralph. "Mechanics of Resonance." *Revision.* Summer 1987, Vol. 10, No. 1.

Achterberg, Jeanne. *Imagery in Healing.* New Science. 1985.

Allesch, Christian G. "A Study of the Influence of Music on Pulse and Respiration Frequency." *Zeitschrift fur experimentelle und angewandte Psychologies,* 1981, Vol. 29.

Alper, Frank, *Exploring Atlantis, Vol. I-III.* Quantum Productions. 1981.

Alper, Harvey P. *Mantra.* State University of New York. 1989.

Andrews, Ted. *Sacred Sounds.* Llewellyn. 1992.

Arya, Pandit Usharbudh. *Mantras and Meditations.* Himalayan Institute. 1981.

Assagioli, Roberto. *Psychosynthesis.* Penguin. 1982.

Baer, Randall & Vicki. *The Crystal Connection.* Harper and Row. 1986.

——————. *Windows of Light.* Harper and Row, 1984.

Beasley, Victor R. *Your Electro-Vibratory Body.* University of the Trees. 1978.

Beaulieu, John. *Music and Sound in the Healing Arts.* Station Hill. 1987.

——————. *Polarity Therapy Workbook.* Beaulieu. 1994.

Benson, Herbert. *The Relaxation Response.* William Morrow. 1975.

Bentov, Itzhak. *Stalking the Wild Pendulum.* Destiny. 1988.

——————. *A Cosmic Book.* Destiny. 1982.

Berendt, Joachim-Ernst. *Nada Brahman: The World is Sound.* Destiny. 1987.

——————. *The Third Ear.* Element. 1988.

Berg, Philip S. *The Power of Aleph Beth, Vols. I and II.* Research Centre of Kabbalah Press. 1988.

Bernhardt, Patrick. *The Secret Music of the Soul.* Image. 1991.

Bernstein, Leonard. *The Unanswered Question.* Harvard University. 1976.

Bird, Christopher and Peter Tompkins. *The Secret Life of Plants.* Harper & Row. 1973.

——————. *Secrets of the Soil.* Harper & Row. 1990.

Birosik, Patti Jean. *The New Age Music Guide.* Macmillan. 1989.

Blair, Lawrence. *Rhythms of Vision.* Schocken. 1976.

Blofield, John. *Mantras: Secret Words of Power.* Mandala. 1977.

Bloom, Pamela. "Soul Music." *New Age Journal.* March/April 1987.

Bonny, Helen and Louis Savary. *Music and Your Mind.* ICM. 1983.

Borg, Susan Gallagher. *Sing Your Body Activity Book.* Resonant Kinesiology. 1993.

Boxhild, Edith Hillman. *Music Therapy for the Developmentally Disabled.* Aspen. 1985.

Boyd, Billy Ray. *Noise and Your Health.* Tatterhill. 1996.

Braden, Gregg. *Awakening to Zero Point.* Radio Bookstore. 1994.

_____. *Walking Between the Worlds.* Radio Bookstore. 1997.

Brewer, Chris & Don Campbell. *Rhythms of Learning.* Zephyr. 1991.

Brody, Sarmad. "Healing and Music: The Viewpoint of Hazrat Inayat Khan." *Healing in Our Time.* 1981, Vol. 1, No.1.

Brody, Robert. "Music Medicine." *Omni,* 1985, Vol, 6, No. 5.

Brown, Barbara. *Supermind.* Harper & Row. 1980.

Bruyere, Rosalyn. *Wheels of Light.* Simon & Schuster. 1994.

Buckland, Raymond. *The Magick of Chant-O-Matics.* Reward. 1978.

Cameron, Julia. *The Vein of Gold.* Putnam. 1996.

Campbell, Don. *Introduction to the Musical Brain.* Magnamusic-Batan. 1983.

_____. *The Roar of Silence.* Quest. 1989.

Campbell, Don, ed. *Music: Physician for Times to Come.* Quest. 1990.

_____. *Music and Miracles.* Quest. 1992.

Chatwin, Bruce. *The Songlines.* Penguin. 1987.

Childress, David Hatcher, ed. *Anti-Gravity and the World Grid.* Adventure. 1987.

Chia, Mantak. *Transform Stress into Vitality.* Healing Tao. 1985.

Chinmoy, Shri. *Kundalini: The Mother Power.* Agni. 1974.

Clynes, Manfred. *Music, Mind and Brain.* Plenum. 1982.

Cooper, Grosvenor and Leonard B. Meyer. *The Rhythmic Structure of Music.* University of Chicago. 1960.

Cott, Jonathan. *Stockhausen.* Simon & Schuster. 1973.

Cousto, Hans. *The Cosmic Octave.* LifeRhythm. 1988.

Crandall, Joanne. *Self-Transformation through Music.* Quest. 1986.

Critchlow, Robert. *Homage to Pythagoras.* Lindisfarn. 1980.

Crowley, Brian and Esther. *Words of Power.* Llewellyn. 1992.

Danielou, Alain. *Music and the Power of Sound.* Inner Traditions International. 1943.

Dannelley, Richard. *Sedona: Beyond the Vortex.* Vortex. 1995.

David-Neel, Alexandra. *Magic and Mystery in Tibet.* Dover. 1971.

Davidson, Gustav. *A Dictionary of Angels*. Free Press. 1967.

Davies, John. *The Psychology of Music*. Stanford University. 1978.

Dreighton, Hold, Gina Palerno and Dina Winter. *Singing and the Etheric Tone*. Anthroposophic. 1991.

Delinkski, Roman. "Interview with La Mont Young." *Interval.* Spring 1984.

DeMohan, Elias. *The Harmonics of Sound, Color and Vibration*. DeVorss. 1994.

Devananda, Swami Vishu. *Meditation and Mantras*. Om Lotus. 1978.

Dewhurst-Maddock, Olivia. *The Book of Sound Therapy*. Fireside. 1993.

Diagram Group. *The Brain*. Pedigree. 1982.

Diallo, Yaya and Mitchell Hall. *The Healing Drum*. Destiny Books. 1989.

Diamond, John. *Your Body Doesn't Lie*. Warner. 1980.

_____. *The Life Energy in Music, Vols. I, II, & III*. Archaeus. 1983, 1986.

Doczi, Gyorgy. *The Power of Limits*. Shambhala. 1981.

Dmitriev, L.B., B.P. Chernov and V.T. Maslov. "Functioning of the Voice Mechanism in Double Voice Touvian Singing." *Foli Phoniat* 35. 1983.

Dupont, Antonia. "Make Music Work for You," *Weight Watcher.* December 1980.

Drake, Michael. *The Shamanic Drum*. Talking Drum. 1991.

Dyczkowski, Mark S.G. *The Doctrine of Vibration*. State University of New York Press. 1987.

Ellingson, Terry Jay. *The Mandala of Sound: Concepts and Sound Structures in Tibetan Ritual Music*. University Microfilms. 1979.

Epstein, Perle. *Kabbalah: The Way of the Jewish Mystic*. Doubleday and Co. Inc. 1978.

Feder, Elaine and Bernard. *The Expressive Arts Therapies*. Prentice Hall. 1981.

Ferguson, Marilyn, ed. "Melanin As Key Organizing Molecule." *Brain/Mind Bulletin.* Aug. 1, 1983, Vol. 8, No. 12/13.

Flatischler, Reinhard. *The Forgotten Power of Rhythm*. Life-Rhythm. 1992.

Finney, Shan. *Noise Pollution.* Impact, 1984.

Fonta, Alberto E. and Julio A. Loschi. "Combined Use of Music with Sound of Heartbeats and Respiratory Rhythm in Psychotherapy." *Acta Psiquiatrica y Psicological de America Latina.* March 1979.

Garfield, Laeh Maggie. *Sound Medicine*. Celestial Arts. 1987.

Gardner, Kay. *Sounding the Inner Landscape: Music as Medicine*. Caduceus. 1990.

Gardner-Gordon, Joy. *The Healing Voice*. The Crossing Press. 1993.

Gerber, Richard. *Vibrational Medicine*. Bear & Co. 1988.

Gilmour, Timothy M., Paul Madaule and Billie Thompson. *About the Tomatis Method*. Listening Center. 1988.

Gimbel, Theo. *Healing through Color*. C.W. Daniel. 1980.

_____. *Form, Sound, Colour and Healing*. C.W. Daniel. 1987.

Goldman, Jonathan. *Healing Sounds*. Element. 1992.

Goldman, Jonathan, Beverly Kempt and Pat Paulson. *Sound Healers Association International Directory and Resource Guide*. Spirit Music. 1995.

Godwin, Joscelyn. *Music, Mysticism and Magic*. Routledge & Kegan Paul. 1986.

_____. *Harmonies of Heaven and Earth*. Inner Traditions International. 1987.

_____. *The Mystery of the Seven Vowels*. Phanes. 1991.

Govinda, Lama Anagarika. *Foundations of Tibetan Mysticism*. Samuel Weiser. 1960.

_____. *Creative Meditation and Multi-Dimensional Consciousness*. Quest. 1976.

Graham, F. Lanier. *The Rainbow Book*. Vintage. 1979.

Gray, William. *The Talking Tree*. Weiser. 1977.

Gunther, Bernard. *Energy, Ecstasy and Your Seven Vital Chakras*. Newcastle. 1983.

Guntheir, Emil. *Music & Your Emotions*. Liveright. 1952.

Halevi, Z'ev ben Shimon. *Adam and the Kabbalistic Tree*. Weiser. 1974.

Halpern, Steven and Louis Savary. *Sound Health*. Harper & Row. 1985.

_____. *Tuning the Human Instrument*. Spectrum. 1980.

Hart, Mickey. *Drumming at the Edge of Magic*. HarperCollins. 1990.

_____. *Planet Drum*. HarperCollins. 1991.

Harvey, Arthur, ed. *Music and Health Sourcebook of Readings*. Eastern Kentucky University. 1989.

Hamel, Peter Michael. *Through Music to the Self*. Shambhala. 1978.

Hampden-Turner, Charles. *Maps of the Mind*. Collier. 1981.

Harner, Michael. *The Way of the Shaman*. Bantam. 1980.

Heline, Corinne. *Color and Muslc in the New Age*. New Age. 1985.

_____. *Music: The Keynote of Human Evolution*. J.F. Rowny. 1965.

Helmhotz, Hermann. *On the Sensations of Tone*. Dover. 1954.

Hero, Barbara. *The Lamdoma Revealed*. Strawberry Hill. 1992.

Hill, Ann. *A Visual Encyclopedia of Unconventional Medicine*. Crown. 1979.

Hills, Christopher. *Nuclear Evolution: Discovery of the Rainbow Body*. University of the Trees. 1972.

Hunt, Roland. *Fragrant and Radiant Healing Symphony*. Starlight. 1937.

Hunt, Valerie. *Infinite Mind*. Malibu. 1996.

_____. *Mind Mastery Meditations*. Malibu. 1997.

Hurtak, J.J. *The Book of Knowledge: The Keys of Enoch.* Academy for Future Science. 1977.

Husemann, Armin. *The Harmony of the Human Body.* Floris Books. 1994.

Hutchinson, Michael. *Megabrain.* Ballantine. 1986.

Hykes, David. *Sonnez Fort: Better Listening and Some Leading Unspoken Questions.* Harmonic Arts. 1984.

Janowitz, Naomi. *The Poetics of Assent.* State University of New York. 1989.

Jansen, Eva Rudy. *Singing Bowls.* Binkey Kok. 1990.

Jansen, Gerd. "Effects of Noise on Psychological States." *Speech and Hearing Association Report.* February 1969.

Jeans, Jean. *Science & Music.* Dover. 1968.

Jenny, Hans. *Cymatics Vols. I & II.* Basilus. 1974.

Jones, Alex. *Seven Mansions of Color.* DeVorss. 1982.

Joy, Brugh W. *Avalanche.* Ballantine. 1990.

Katsch, Shelley and Carol Merle-Fishman. *The Music within You.* Simon & Schuster. 1985.

Kayser, Hans. *Akroasis, the Theory of World Harmonics.* Plowshare. 1970.

Kenyon, Tom. *Brain States.* United States. 1994.

Kenyon, Tom and Virginia Essene. *The Hathor Material.* S.E.E. Publishing Company. 1996.

Keyes, Laurel Elizabeth. *Toning: The Creative Power of the Voice.* DeVorss. 1973.

Khan, Hasrat Inayat. *The Mysticism of Sound; Music: The Power of the Word; Cosmic Language [a compendium].* Barry & Rockcliff. 1962.

Khan, Pir Vilayat. *Towards the One.* Lama Foundation. 1971.

Kneutgen, Johannes. "On the Effects of Lullabies." *Zetschrift fur experimentelle und angewandte Psychologie.* 1970, Vol. I.

Krieger, Dolores. *The Therapeutic Touch.* Prentice Hall. 1979.

_____. *Foundations of Holistic Health Nursing Practices.* J.P. Lippincott. 1981.

Landreth, Janet E. and Hobart F. "Effects of Music on Physiological Response." *Journal of Research in Music Education.* 1974, Vol. 22.

Leonard, George. *The Silent Pulse.* E.P. Dutton. 1978.

Levarie, Siegmund and Ernst Levy. *Tone.* Kent State. 1968.

Levin, Flora R. *The Manual of Harmonics.* Phanes. 1994.

Levin, Theodore. *A Note about Harmonic Music.* Harmonic Arts. 1984.

_____. *Tuva, Voices from the Center of Asia.* Smithsonian. 1990.

_____. *The Hundred Thousand Fools of God.* Indiana University. 1996.

Lewis, Robert C. *The Sacred Word and Its Creative Overtones.* Rosecrucian. 1986.

Lieberman, Jacob. *Light: Medicine of the Future.* Bear & Co. 1991.

Lingerman, Hal A. *The Healing Energies of Music.* Quest. 1983.

Linklater, Kristin. *Freeing the Natural Voice.* Drama. 1976.

Lloyd, Llewellyn S. and Hugh Boyle. *Intervals, Scales and Temperament.* St. Martin's Press. 1978.

Lundin, Robert W. *An Objective Psychology of Music.* Ronald Press. 1967.

Maclagan, David. *Creation Myths.* Thames and Hudson. 1977.

Madaukem, Paul. *When Listening Comes Alive.* Moulin. 1993.

Malekskey, Gale. "Music to Get Cured By." *Prevention.* Oct. 1983.

Maman, Fabian. *From the Stars to the Acupuncture Points.* Tama-Do. 1991.

Maple, Eric. *Incantations and Words of Power.* Samuel Weiser. 1974.

Manners, Peter Guy. *Cymatic Therapy.* Bretforton. 1976.

—————————. *The Future of Cymatic Therapy: Sound and Vibratory Pattern Research.* Bretforton. 1976.

—————————. *The Origins of Music.* Bretforton. 1980.

Marks, Kate. *Circle of Song: Songs, Chants and Dances for Ritual and Celebration.* Full Circle Press. 1993.

Mathieu, W.A. *The Listening Book.* Shambhala. 1991.

—————————. *The Musical Life.* Shambhala. 1994.

McClain, Ernest G. *The Pythagorean Plato.* Nicolas Hays. 1978.

—————————. *The Myth of Invariance.* Nicolas Hays. 1976.

McClellan, Randall. *The Healing Forces of Music: History, Theory and Practice.* Element. 1988.

Metzner, Jim. *Chanted Blessings in Disguise.* Parabola. 1989.

Meyers, John. *Human Rhythms and the Psychobiology of Entrainment.* Bell Communication. 1987.

Merrit, Stephanie. *Mind, Music and Imagery.* Penguin. 1990.

Mora, Kay. *The Kay Mora Sound Trance.* Spirit. 1983.

Morris, Scot. "Secret Mantras." *Omni.* 1984, Vol. 6, No. 4.

Motoyama, Hiroshi. *Theories of Chakras: Bridge to Higher Consciousness.* Quest. 1981.

—————————. "The Functional Relationship between Yoga Asanas and Acupuncture Meridians." *Healing in Our Times.* Nov. 6, 1981.

Muktananda, Swami. *Where Are You Going?* SYDA. 1981.

Murchie, Guy. *Music of the Spheres.* Dover. 1967.

Murthy, Padma. "Therapeutic Value of South Indian Music." *International Journal of Music, Dance and Art Therapy.* April 1988.

Neal, Viola Petit and Shafica Karagulla. *Through the Curtain.* DeVorss. 1983.

Newby, Hayes A. *Audiology.* Meredith. 1964.

Newham, Paul. *The Singing Cure.* Shambhala. 1993.

Newman, Frederick R. *Mouth Sounds.* Workman. 1980.

Noll, Michael. *Astrology and Music.* NESH Meeting. Dec. 14, 1986.

Oates, David John. *Reverse Speech, the Hidden Messages in Human Communication.* Knowledge Systems, Inc. 1991.

Ostrander, Sheila and Lynn Schroeder. *Superlearning.* Putnam. 1982.

Pearsall, Paul. *Superimmunity.* McGraw-Hill. 1987.

Pierce, John R. *The Science of Musical Sounds.* Scientific Books. 1983.

Polon, Martin. "Db's Can Be Hazardous to Your Health." Re-elp. 1980.

Ponce, Charles. *The Kabbalah.* Quest. 1972.

Pond, Dale. *Keeley's Secrets.* Vibratory Physics. 1990.

Powers, William K. *Sacred Language.* University of Oklahoma. 1986.

Prophet, Elizabeth Claire. "Sound: Life's Integrated Phenomenon." Summit University. 1981.

Purce, Jill. "Sound in Mind & Body." *Resurgence. March 1986,* No. 115.

Radha, Swami Sivananda. *Mantras: Words of Power.* Timeless. 1980.

Rael, Joseph. *Being and Vibration.* Council Oak Books. 1993.

Rael, Joseph and Lindsay Sutton. *Tracks of Dancing Light.* Element. 1993.

Ram Dass. *Be Here Now.* Lama Foundation. 1971.

Raphael, Katrina. *Crystal Enlightenment.* Aurora. 1985.

————————. *Crystal Healing.* Aurora. 1987.

————————. *Crystal Transmission.* Aurora. 1990.

Retallack, Dorothy. *The Sound of Music and Plants.* DeVorss. 1973.

Richmann, Howard. "Entrainment for Pain Reduction." *International Journal of Music, Dance and Art Therapy.* April 1988.

Ristad, Eloise. *A Soprano in Her Head.* Real People. 1982.

Roger, John. *Inner Worlds of Meditation.* Baraka. 1976.

Roney-Dougal, Serena. *Where Science and Magic Meet.* Element Books Limited. 1991.

Rouget, Gilbert. *Music and Trance.* University of Chicago. 1985.

Rudyhar, Dane. *The Magic of Tone and the Art of Music.* Shambhala. 1983.

————————. *The Rebirth of Hindu Music.* Samuel Weiser. 1979.

Saraswati, Swami Yogeshwaranand. *Science of Divine Sound.* Yog Niketan. 1984.

Scarantino, Barbara Anne. *Music Power.* Dodd, Mead & Co. 1987.

Scott, Cyril. *Music.* Aquarian. 1993.

Schaefer, Murray R. *The Tunings of the World.* Knopf. 1977.

Schellberg, Dirk. *Didgeridoo.* Binkey Kok. 1993.

Schwartz, Jack. *Human Energy Systems.* E.F. Dutton. 1980.

SCWL Research Report. *Comparative Studies and Other Documentation on the Effect of Subliminal Suggestion.* Joe Land. 1985.

Seashore, Carl E. *Psychology of Music.* Dover. 1938.

Serjak, Cynthia. *Music and the Cosmic.* Pastoral. 1987.

Shannanoff-Khalsa, D.S. and Yogi Bhajan. "Sound-Current Therapy and Self-Healing: The Ancient Science of Nad and Mantra Yoga." *International Journal of Music, Dance and Art Therapy.* April 1988.

Shulman, Lee and Joyce, and Gerald Rafferty. *Subliminal.* InfoBooks. 1991.

Silbey, Uma. *The Complete Crystal Guidebook.* U-Read. 1986.

Siegel, Jane and William. "Categorical Perceptions of Tonal Intervals." *Perception & Psychophysics.* Vol. 21(5).

Singh, Kirpal. *Crown of Life.* Shabt. 1970.

_____. *Naam or Word.* Ruhani Satsang. 1960.

Singh, Ranjie N. *Self-Healing.* Health Psychology. 1997.

Skille, Olav. "The Effects of Vibro-Acoustic Treatment on 4 Rheumatic Patients." *International Journal of Music, Dance and Art Therapy.* April 1988.

Smith, Huston. *Requiem for a Faith.* Hartley Films. 1980.

Solomont, Elide M. *You Are Who You Hate.* Vantage Press Inc. 1995.

Spintge, Ralph and Droh, Roland. *Music in Medicine.* Hoffman LaRoche. 1985.

Spintge, Ralph and Droh, Roland, eds. *Music Medicine.* MMB Music. 1992.

Statnekov, Daniel K. *Animated Earth.* North Atlantic Books. 1987.

Steiger, Brad. *Charms, Chants and Crystal Magic for the New Age.* Inner Light. 1987.

Steiner, Rudolf. *The Inner Nature of Music and the Experience of Tone.* Anthroposophic. 1983.

Stewart, R.J. *Music and the Elemental Psyche.* Destiny. 1987.

Storr, Anthony. *Music and the Mind.* Ballentine. 1992.

Sui, Choa Kos. *Advanced Pranic Healing.* Inner Studies. 1992.

Sullivan, Anita T. *The Seventh Dragon: The Riddle of Equal Temperament.* Metamorphous. 1985.

Tame, David. *The Secret Power of Music.* Destiny. 1984.

Tansley, David V. *Radionics & the Subtle Anatomy of Man.* Health Science. 1972.

Taylor, Eldon. *Subliminal Communication.* JAR. 1986.

Tomatis, A.A. *Education and Dyslexia.* AAIPP. 1978.

_____. *The Conscious Ear*. Station Hill Press. 1991.

_____. *The Ear and Language*. Moulin Publishing. 1996.

Twitchell, Paul. *The Spiritual Notebook*. Illuminated Way. 1972.

Twyman, James. *Emissary of Light*. Aslan. 1996.

Vennard, William. *Singing*. Carl Fischer. 1967.

Wafer, Jim. *Vibrational Healing with the Australian Aboriginal Didgeridoo*. Inma-Ku. 1997.

Walcott, Ronald. "The Choomij of Mongolia: A Spectral Analysis of Overtone Singing." *Selected Reports in Ethnomusicology.* 1974, Vol. II, No. 1.

Watson, Andrew and Nevil Drury. *Healing Music*. Nature & Health. 1987.

Webster, Cecily. "Relaxation, Music and Cardiology: The Physiological and Psychological Consequences of Their Interrelation." *Australian Occupational Therapy Journal.* January. 1973.

Weed, Joseph J. *Wisdom of the Mystic Masters*. Parker. 1973.

Wein, Bibi. "Body and Soul Music." *American Health.* April 1987.

White, Harvey and Donald. *Physics of Music*. Holt, Rinehart & Winston. 1980.

Wier, Dennis R. *Trance: From Magic to Technology*. Trans Media Inc. 1996.

Winckel, Fritz. *Music, Sound and Sensation*. Dover. 1967.

Winter, Arthur and Ruth. "Music to Give Your Mind a Workout." *New Woman.* October 1987.

Winter, Dan. *Sacred Geometry: The Alphabet of the Heart*. Crystal Hill. 1992.

Winn, James Anderson. *Unsuspected Eloquence*. Yale. 1981.

Winnston, Shirley Rabb. *Music As the Bridge*. ARE. 1972.

Zukav, Gary. *The Dancing Wu Li Masters*. Bantam. 1979.

Biography of Jonathan Goldman

Jonathan Goldman is an internationally known author, musician, chant master and teacher. Pioneering the field of harmonics, he has studied with masters of sound from the scientific and spiritual traditions and is empowered by the chant master of the Drepung Loseling Monastery to teach sacred Tibetan overtone chanting. He has been initiated into many different spiritual traditions and is a conscious channel for Shamael, Angel of Sound. He has an M.A. in the Uses of Sound and Music for Healing.

Jonathan is the author of several books, including *Healing Sounds*, considered a landmark in the sound healing arena, and *The Lost Chord*, a novel. His recordings include: *Dolphin Dreams, Trance Tara*, the best selling *Chakra Chants*, winner of the 1999 Visionary Awards for "Best Healing-Meditation Album" and "Album of the Year", and his most recent CD, *The Lost Chord*

Jonathan is the director of the Sound Healers Association and president of Spirit Music in Boulder, Colorado. He travels throughout the world empowering others with the ability to create and use healing and transformational sounds.

Jonathan is available for lectures, workshops and seminars. For more information about his teaching and his transformational sounds, contact him via:

Spirit Music, P.O. Box 2240, Boulder, CO 80306 USA
Phone: (303) 443-8181
Fax: (303) 443-6023
Email:soundheals@aol.com
Website: www.healingsounds.com

THE EXPLORER RACE SERIES

ZOOSH THROUGH ROBERT SHAPIRO

Superchannel Robert Shapiro can communicate with any personality anywhere and anywhen. He has been a professional channel for over twenty-five years and channels with an exceptionally clear and profound connection.

The Origin...
The Purpose...The Future...of Humanity

If you have ever questioned about who you really are, why you are here as part of humanity on this miraculous planet and what it all means, these books in the Explorer Race series can begin to supply the answers—the answers to these and other questions about the mystery and enigma of physical life on Earth.

These answers come from beings who speak through superchannel Robert Shapiro, beings who range from particle personalities to the Mother of all Beings and the thirteen Ssjooo, from advisors to the Creator of our universe to the generators of precreation energies. The scope, the immensity, the mind-boggling infinitude of these chronicles by beings who live in realms beyond our imagination, will hold you enthralled. Nothing even close to the magnitude of the depth and power of this all-encompassing, expanded picture of reality has ever been published.

This amazing story of the greatest adventure of all time and creation is the story of the Explorer Race, of which humans are a small but important percentage. The Explorer Race is a group of souls whose journeys resulted in incarnations in this loop of time on planet Earth, where, bereft of any memory of our immortal selves and most of our heart energy, we came to learn compassion, to learn to take responsibility for the consequences of our actions and to solve creation's previously unsolvable dilemma of negativity. We humans have found a use for negativity—we use it for lust for life and adventure, curiosity and creativity, for doing the undoable. And in a few years we will go out to the stars with our insatiable drive and ability to respond to change, and begin to inspire the benign but stagnant civilizations out there to expand and change and grow, which will eventually result in the change and expansion of all creation.

Once you understand the saga of the Explorer Race and what the success of the Explorer Race Experiment means to the totality of creation, you will be proud to be a human and to know that you are a vital component of the greatest story ever told—a continuing drama whose adventure continues far into the future.

the

EXPLORER RACE

Zoosh, End-Time Historian
through Robert Shapiro

Book 1...
The Explorer Race

You individuals reading this are truly a result of the genetic experiment on Earth. You are beings who uphold the principles of the Explorer Race. The information in this book is designed to show you who you are and give you an evolutionary understanding of your past that will help you now. The key to empowerment in these days is to not know everything about your past, but to know that which will help you now.

Your souls have been here for a while on Earth and have been trained in Earthlike conditions. This education has been designed so that you would have the ability to explore all levels of responsibility—results, effects and consequences—and take on more responsibilities.

Your number one function right now is your status of Creator apprentice, which you have achieved through years and lifetimes of sweat. You are constantly being given responsibilities by the Creator that would normally be things that Creator would do. The responsibility and the destiny of the Explorer Race is not only to explore, but to create. SOFTCOVER 574P.

$25⁰⁰   ISBN 0-929385-38-1

Chapter Titles:

THE HISTORY OF THE EXPLORER RACE
• The Genetic Experiment on Earth
• Influences of the Zodiac
• The Heritage from Early Civilizations
• Explorer Race Time Line, Part 1
• Explorer Race Time Line, Part 2
• The Experiment That Failed
GATHERING THE PARTS
• The ET in You: Physical Body
• The ET in You: Emotion and Thought
• The ET in You: Spirit
THE JOY, THE GLORY AND THE CHALLENGE OF SEX
• Emotion Lost: Sexual Addiction in Zeta History
• Sex, Love and Relationships
• Sexual Violence on Earth
• The Third Sex: The Neutral Binding Energy
• The Goddess Energy: The Soul of Creation
ET PERSPECTIVES
• Origin of the Species: A Sirian Perception
• An Andromedan Perspective on the Earth
  Experiment
• The Perspective of Orion Past on Their Role
• Conversation with a Zeta

BEHIND THE SCENES
• The Order: Its Origin and Resolution
• The White Brotherhood, the Illuminati, the New
  Dawn and the Shadow Government
• Fulfilling the Creator's Destiny
• The Sirian Inheritors of Third-Dimensional Earth
TODAY AND TOMORROW
• The Explorer Race Is Ready
• Coming of Age in the Fourth Dimension
• The True Purpose of Negative Energy
• The Challenge of Risking Intimacy
• Etheric Gene-Splicing and the Neutral Particle
• Material Mastery and the New Safety
• The Sterilization of Planet Earth
THE LOST PLANETS
• The Tenth Planet: The Gift of Temptation
• The Eleventh Planet: The Undoer, Key to
  Transformation
• The Twelfth Planet: Return of the Heart Energy
THE HEART OF HUMANKIND
• Moving Beyond the Mind
• Retrieving Heart Energy
• The Creator's Mission and the Function of the
  Human Race

Book 2...
ETs and the EXPLORER RACE

n this book, Robert channels Joopah, a Zeta Reticulan now in he ninth dimension, who continues the story of the great experiment—the Explorer Race—from the perspective of his civilization. The Zetas would have been humanity's future selves had not humanity re-created the past and changed the future.

SOFTCOVER 237P.
$14 95 ISBN 0-929385-79-9

Joopah, Zoosh and others through Robert Shapiro

Chapter Titles:

- The Great Experiment: Earth Humanity
- ETs Talk to Contactees
- Becoming One with Your Future Self
- ET Interaction with Humanity
- UFOs and Abductions
- The True Nature of the Grays
- Answering Questions in Las Vegas
- UFO Encounters in Sedona

- Joopah, in Transit, Gives an Overview and Helpful Tools
- We Must Embrace the Zetas
- Roswell, ETs and the Shadow Government
- ETs: Friend or Foe?
- ET Presence within Earth and Human Genetics
- Creating a Benevolent Future
- Bringing the Babies Home

Book 3...ORIGINS and the NEXT 50 YEARS

This volume has so much information about who we are and where we came from—the source of male and female beings, the war of the sexes, the beginning of the linear mind, feelings, the origin of souls—it is a treasure trove. Then in addition there is a section that relates to our near future—how the rise of global corporations and politics affects our future, how to use benevolent magic as a force of creation and then how we will go out to the stars and affect other civilizations. Astounding information.

SOFTCOVER 339P.
$14 95 ISBN 0-929385-95-0

ORIGINS and the NEXT 50 YEARS

Zoosh, End-Time Historian through Robert Shapiro

Chapter Titles:

THE ORIGINS OF EARTH RACES
- Our Creator and Its Creation
  The White Race and the Andromedan Linear Mind
  The Asian Race, the Keepers of Zeta Vertical Thought
  The African Race and Its Sirius/Orion Heritage
  The Fairy Race and the Native Peoples of the North
  The Australian Aborigines, Advisors of the Sirius System
  The Return of the Lost Tribe of Israel
  The Body of the Child, a Pleiadian Heritage
  Creating Sexual Balance for Growth
  The Origin of Souls
THE NEXT 50 YEARS
  The New Corporate Model
  The Practice of Feeling

- Benevolent Magic
- Future Politics
- A Visit to the Creator of All Creators
- Approaching the One
APPENDIX
- The Body of Man/The Body of Woman
ORIGINS OF THE CREATOR
- Beginning This Creation
- Creating with Core Resonances
- Jesus, the Master Teacher
- Recent Events in Explorer Race History
- The Origin of Creator
- On Zoosh, Creator and the Explorer Race
- Fundamentals of Applied 3D Creationism

EXPLORER RACE

CREATORS AND FRIENDS
THE MECHANICS OF CREATION

Creators and Zoosh
through Robert Shapiro

Book 4...CREATORS and FRIEND
The Mechanics of Creation

Now that you have a greater understanding of who you are in th larger sense, it is necessary to remind you of where you came from the true magnificence of your being, to have some of your true peer talk to you. You must understand that you are creators in training and yet you were once a portion of Creator. One could certainly say without being magnanimous, that you are still a portion of Creato yet you are training for the individual responsibility of being a cre ator, to give your Creator a coffee break.

This book will give you peer consultation. it will allow you to understand the vaster qualitie and help you remember the nature of the desires that drive any creator, the responsibilities t which that creator must answer, the reaction any creator must have to consequences and th ultimate reward of any creator. This book will help you appreciate all of the above and more I hope you will enjoy it and understand that maybe more will follow. SOFTCOVER 435P.

$**19**95 ISBN 0-891824-01-?

Chapter Titles:

- Andastinn, Prototype of Insect Beings
- Kazant, a Timekeeper
- Founders of Sirius, Creators of Humanoid Forms
- A Teacher of Buddha and Time Master's Assistant
- Designers of Human Physiology
- Avatar of Sea Creatures; and Quatsika, Messenger for the Dimension Makers
- The Empath Creator of Seventeen Planets
- Shapemaker of Portals
- Creator of the Inverse Universe, Our Creator's Creator
- Creator of the Void, Preamble to Individuality
- The Tornado-Shaped Creator of Creators
- The Center of Creation
- The Heart Council
- Creators of Gold Light and White Light
- Creator Talks About Itself and the Explorer Race
- Creator Talks About Friends

- Creator Speaks of the Stuff of Creation
- Creator Discusses Successes and the Outworking of Negativity
- Synchronizer of Physical Reality and Dimensions
- Master of Maybe
- Master of Frequencies and Octaves
- Spirit of Youthful Exuberance
- Master of Imagination
- Zoosh, the End-Time Historian
- Master of Feeling
- Master of Plasmic Energy
- Master of Discomfort Speaks of Himself and the Explorer Race
- Master of Discomfort Discusses Light Transference

Appendix: The Lucifer Gene

Book 5...
PARTICLE PERSONALITIES

All around you are the most magical and mystical beings. They are too small for you to see as single individuals, but in groups you know them as the physical matter of your daily life. These particles remember where they have been and what they have done in their long lives. We hear from some of them in this extraordinary book. SOFTCOVER 237P.

$14⁹⁵ ISBN 0-929385-97-7

Chapter Titles:

- A Particle of Gold
  The Model Maker: The Clerk
  The Clerk; a Mountain Lion Particle; a Particle of Liquid Light; and an Ice Particle
- A Particle of Rose Quartz from a Floating Crystal City
- A Particle of Uranium, Earth's Mind
- A Particle of the Great Pyramid's Capstone
- A Particle of the Dimensional Boundary between Orbs

- A Particle of Healing Energy
- A Particle of Courage Circulating through Earth
- A Particle of the Sun
- A Particle of Ninth-Dimensional Fire
- A Particle of Union
- A Particle of the Gold Lightbeing beyond the Orbs
- A Particle of the Tenfold Wizard
- A Particle of This Creator

Book 6...EXPLORER RACE
and BEYOND

With a better idea of how creation works, we go back to the Creator's advisors and receive deeper and more profound explanations of the roots of the Explorer Race. The liquid Domain and the Double Diamond portal share lessons given to the roots on their way to meet the Creator of this Universe and finally the roots speak of their origins and their incomprehensibly long journey here. SOFTCOVER 360P.

$14⁹⁵ ISBN 1-891824-06-6

Chapter Titles:

- Creator of Pure Feelings and Thoughts, One Circle of Creation
- The Liquid Domain
- The Double-Diamond Portal
- About the Other 93% of the Explorer Race
- Synchronizer of Physical Reality and Dimensions
- The Master of Maybe
- Master of Frequencies and Octaves
- Spirit of Youthful Enthusiasm (Junior) and Master of Imagination
- Zoosh
- The Master of Feeling

- The Master of Plasmic Energy
- The Master of Discomfort
- The Story-Gathering Root Being from the Library of Light/Knowledge
- The Root Who Fragmented from a Living Temple
- The First Root Returns
- Root Three, Companion of the Second Root
- The Temple of Knowledge & the Giver of Inspiration
- The Voice Historian, Who Provided the First Root
- Creator of All That Is

Coming from Light Technology Publishing

BOOKS 7-13... COMING SOON

Book 7...EXPLORER RACE: the COUNCIL of CREATORS

THE EXPLORER RACE

COUNCIL O CREATOR

AND ZOOSH THRO
ROBERT SHAPI

The 13 core members of the Council of Creators discuss their adventures in coming to awareness of themselves and their journeys on the way to the Council on this level. They discuss the advice and oversight they offer to all creators, including the creator of this local universe. These beings are wise, witty and joyous, and their stories of Love's Creation creates an expansion of our concepts as we realize that we live in an expanded, multiple-level reality. SOFTCOVER 237P.

Chapter Titles:
$14⁹⁵ ISBN 1-891824-13-9

- Specialist in Colors, Sounds and Consequences of Actions
- Specialist in Membranes that Separate and Auditory Mechanics
- Specialist in Sound Duration
- Explanation from Unknown Member of Council
- Specialist in Spatial Reference
- Specialist in Gaps and Spaces
- Specialist in Divine Intervention
- Specialist in Synchronicity and Timing

- Specialist in Hope
- Specialist in Honor
- Specialist in Variety
- Specialist in Mystical Connection between Animals and Humans
- Specialist in Change
- Specialist in the Present Moment
- Council Spokesperson and Specialist in Auxiliary Life Forms

Book 8...EXPLORER RACE and ISIS

THE EXPLORER RACE

ISIS

AND ZOOSH THROUGH
ROBERT SHAPIRO

This is an amazing book. It has priestess training, Shamanic training, Isis adventures with Explorer Race beings—before Earth and on Earth—and an incredibly expanded explanation of the dynamics of the Explorer Race. Isis is the prototypal loving, nurturing, guiding feminine being, the focus of feminine energy. She has the ability to expand limited thinking without making people with limited beliefs feel uncomfortable. She is a fantastic storyteller and all of her stories are teaching stories. If you care about who you are, why you are here, where you are going and what life is all about—pick up this book. You won't lay it down until you ar through, and then you will want more. SOFTCOVER 317P.

Chapter Titles:
$14⁹⁵ ISBN 1-891824-11-

- The Biography of Isis
- The Adventurer
- Soul Colors and Shapes
- Creation Mechanics
- Creation Mechanics and Personal Anecdotes

- The Insects' Form and Fairies
- Orion and Application to Earth
- Goddess Section
- Who Is Isis?
- Priestess/Feminine Mysteries

Book 9...EXPLORER RACE and JESUS

The immortal personality who lived the life we know as Jesus, along with his students and friends, describes with clarity and love his life and teaching on Earth 2000 years ago. These beings lovingly offer their experiences of the events that happened then and of Jesus' time-traveling adventures, especially to other planets and to the nineteenth and twentieth centuries, which he called the time of the machines—the time of the troubles. So heartwarming and interesting you won't want to put it down.

Chapter Titles:

$14⁹⁵ ISBN 1-891824-14-7

- Jesus' Core Being, His People and the Interest in Earth of Four of Them
- Jesus' Life on Earth
- Jesus' Home World, Their Love Creations and the Four Who Visited Earth
- The "Facts" of Jesus' Life Here, His Future Return
- The Teachings and Travels
- A Student's Time with Jesus and His Tales of Jesus' Time Travels
- The Shamanic Use of the Senses

- The Child Student Who Became a Traveling Singer-Healer
- Other Journeys and the Many Disguises
- Jesus' Autonomous Parts, His Bloodline and His Plans
- Learning to Invite Matter to Transform Itself
- Inviting Water, Singing Colors
- Learning to Teach Usable Skills
- Learning about Different Cultures and People
- The Role of Mary Magdalene, a Romany
- Traveling and Teaching People How to Find Things

Book 10...EXPLORER RACE: EARTH HISTORY and LOST CIVILIZATIONS EXPLAINED

Zoosh reveals that our planet Earth did not originate in this solar system, but the water planet we live on was brought here from Sirius 65 million years ago. Anomalous archaeological finds and the various ET cultures who founded what we now call lost civilizations are explained with such storytelling skill by Speaks of Many Truths that you feel you were there!

Chapter Titles:

$14⁹⁵ ISBN 1-891824-20-1

- Lost Civilizations of Planet Earth in Sirius
- Ancient Artifacts Explained
- Ancient Visitors and Immortal Personalities
- Before and after Earth Was Moved to This Solar System from Sirius
- The Long Journey of Jehovah's Ship, from Orion to Sirius to Earth
- Jehovah Creates Human Beings
- Beings from the Future Academy
- Sumer
- Nazca Lines
- Easter Island
- Laetoli Footprints

- Egypt and Cats
- Three More Civilizations
- Medicine Wheels
- Stonehenge
- Carnac in Brittany
- Egypt
- China
- Tibet and Japan
- Siberia
- Natural Foods/Sacrament of Foods
- SSG's Time-Traveling Interference in Israel Imperils Middle East: How to Resolve It

Book 11...EXPLORER RACE: ET VISITORS to EARTH SPEAK

Even as you are searching the sky for extraterrestrials and their space ships, ETs are here on planet Earth—they are stranded, visiting, exploring, studying the culture, healing the Earth of trauma brought on by irresponsible mining or researching the history of Christianity over the last 2000 years. Some are in human guise, some are in spirit form, some look like what we call animals as they come from the species' home planet and interact with those of their fellow beings that we have labeled cats or cows or elephants. Some are brilliant cosmic mathematicians with a sense of humor presently living here as penguins; some are fledgling diplomats training for future postings on Earth when we have ET embassies here. In this book, these fascinating beings share their thoughts, origins and purposes for being here.

$14⁹⁵ ISBN 1-891824-28

Chapter Titles:

- Stranded Sirian Lightbeing Observes Earth for 800 Years
- An Orion Being Talks about Life on Earth as a Human
- Sensient Redwood
- Quah Earth Religion Researcher
- Visitor to Earth Talks about Pope Pius XII
- Observer Helps Cats Accomplish Their Purpose: Initiating
- A Warrior of Light, the Ultimate Ally
- Penguins: Humorous Mathematicians
- Xri from the Ninth Dimension
- Nurturing the Birth Cord
- Sixth Dimensional Cha-Cha Dances with Humans
- Starlight for Regeneration of Earth's Crystal Veins
- Starlight for Regeneration of Earth's Crystal Veins
- ET Resource Specialists Map and Heal Planetary Bodies
- The Creation and Preparation of the Resource Specialists' Ships Part 3
- Future Zeta Diplomat Learns to Communicate with Humans
- Warrior of Light
- Sirius Water-Being—A Bridge between ETs and Humans
- The Rock-Being Here to Experience Movement
- We Need Benevolent Alien Implants to Go to the Stars
- Ketchin-sa—ET in Dog Form
- Balanced Beings Attempt to Remove Earth Beings' Discomfort

Book 12...EXPLORER RACE and THE FUTURE-ANCHORED TIME LINE

The opportunity to change the way you live is not only close at hand, it is with you right now. Some of you have felt a change in the air, as you say, the winds of change. Sometimes you can almost taste it or smell it or feel it. And other times it is ephemeral—hard to grasp. It is the ephemeral quality that can help you to know that the good thing that is out of your reach has to do with the future time line. The future time line is also an experience line. It is a sensation line. It is associated with the way your physical body communicates to you and others. It is a way of increasing your sensitivity to your own needs and the needs of others in a completely safe and protected way so that you can respond more quickly and accurately to those needs and appreciate the quality of life around you, much of which you miss because the old time line discourages you from observing. It encourages you to study and understand, but it discourages you from feeling. And it is feeling that is the ultimate answer to your discomforts as well as the pathway to true benevolent insight and fulfillment. When you read this book, know that it is intended to give you the gift of ease that comes with the simpler path, the less complicated path and the path without attachments.

14^{95} ISBN 1-891824-26-0

Chapter Titles:

- Zero Four
- Time Traveler
- Fluid of Time
- Ordinator of Souls
- Energy Three
- Mother of All Beings

Book 13...EXPLORER RACE: THE ULTIMATE UFO BOOK

This is a UFO book with a twist. The beings who channeled through Robert are the ET beings who were on the ships with humans in the famous case files—Betty and Barney Hill, Betty Andreasson, Travis Walton and many, many others. Here is a completely different perspective on the reality of off-planet/Earth-human interactions. As the various beings describe who they are, your understanding of our neighbors in space will expand.

14^{95} ISBN 1-891824-19-8

Chapter Titles:

- ET Contacts
- Daughter of Isis
- Zeta Coordinator
- People of Zeta
- Roswell
- The True Purpose of the Zetas
- Andromedan Diplomatic Liaison to the Zetas and the Parent Race
- Parent Race of Zeta ET Contacts
- Faces of the Visitors
- Visitors' Book & Sirian Mapper
- Bears, Meditation Beings
- Criminals, the Vega Star System and Microbes
- Botucatu, Brazil: Joao and the Andromedans
- Pascagoula, Mississippi: Hickson and Parker
- Guardians at Pascagoula
- The Andromedans: A Tale of a Minister
- Andromedans in Mexico and Professor Hernandez

THE ANCIENT SECRET OF THE FLOWER OF LIFE

DRUNVALO MELCHIZEDEK

Drunvalo Melchizedek's life experience reads like an encyclopedia of break-throughs in human endeavor. He studied physics and art at the University of California at Berkeley, but he feels that his most important education came after college. In the last 25 years, he has studied with over 70 teachers from all belief systems and religious understandings.

For some time now, he has been bringing his vision to the world through the Flower of Life program and the Mer-Ka-Ba meditation. This teaching encompasses every area of human understanding, explores the development of mankind from ancient civilizations to the present time and offers clarity regarding the world's state of consciousness and what is needed for a smooth and easy transition into the 21st century.

VOLUME I

Once, all life in the universe knew the Flower of Life as the creation pattern, the geometrical design leading us into and out of physical existence. Then from a very high state of consciousness, we fell into darkness, the secret hidden for thousands of years, encoded in the cells of all life.

Now we are rising from the darkness and a new dawn is streaming through the windows of perception. This book is one of those windows. Drunvalo Melchizedek presents in text and graphics the Flower of Life Workshop, illuminating the mysteries of how we came to be.

Sacred geometry is the form beneath our being and points to a divine order in our reality. We can follow that order from the invisible atom to the infinite stars, finding ourselves at each step. The information here is one path, but between the lines and drawings lie the feminine gems of intuitive understanding. **SOFTCOVER 228P.**

$**25**^{00}$ ISBN 1-891824-17-1

Chapter Titles:

- Remembering Our Ancient Past
- The Secret of the Flower Unfolds
- The Darker Side of Our Present and Past
- The Aborted Evolution of Consciousness and the Creation of the Christ Grid
- Egypt's Role in the Evolution of Consciousness
- The Geometries of the Human Body
- The Significance of Shape and Structure
- When Evolution Crashed, and the Christ Grid Arose
- The Measuring Stick of the Universe: The Human Body and Its Geometries
- Reconciling the Fibonacci-Binary Polarity

VOLUME II

The sacred Flower of Life pattern, the primary geometric generator of all physical form, is explored in even more depth in this volume, the second half of the famed Flower of Life workshop. The proportions of the human body, the nuances of human consciousness, the sizes and distances of the stars, planets and moons, even the creations of humankind, are all shown to reflect their origins in this beautiful and divine image. Through an intricate and detailed geometrical mapping, Drunvalo Melchizedek shows how the seemingly simple design of the Flower of Life contains the genesis of our entire third-dimensional existence.

From the pyramids and mysteries of Egypt to the new race of Indigo children, Drunvalo presents the sacred geometries of the Reality and the subtle energies that shape our world. We are led through a divinely inspired labyrinth of science and stories, logic and coincidence, on a path of remembering where we come from and the wonder and magic of who we are.

Finally, for the first time in print, Drunvalo shares the instructions for the Mer-Ka-Ba meditation, step-by-step techniques for the re-creation of the energy field of the evolved human, which is the key to ascension and the next dimensional world. If done from love, this ancient process of breathing prana opens up for us a world of tantalizing possibility in this dimension, from protective powers to the healing of oneself, of others and even of the planet. You may discover a memory or a fleeting reflection of yourself in the following topics:

- The unfolding of the third informational system
- Whispers from our ancient heritage
- Unveiling the Mer-Ka-Ba mediation
- Using your Mer-Ka-Ba
- Connecting to the levels of self
- Two cosmic experiments
- What we may expect in the forthcoming dimensional shift

SOFTCOVER 228P.

$25.00 ISBN 1-891824-21-X

Chapter Titles:

- **Spirit and Sacred Geometry**
- **The Left Eye of Horus Mystery School**
- **Ancient Influences on Our Modern World**
- **The Mer-Ka-Ba, the Human Lightbody**
- **The Mer-Ka-Ba Geometries and Meditation**
- **The Mer-Ka-Ba and the Siddhis**
- **Love and Healing**
- **The Three Levels of the Self**
- **Duality Transcended**
- **The Dimensional Shift**
- **The New Children**